ME AND YOU
AND POEMS 2

ME AND YOU AND POEMS 2

Collected and illustrated by *Rolf Harris*

From an original compilation by
Michael Johnstone

KNIGHT BOOKS
Hodder and Stoughton

A catalogue record for this title is available from the British Library

ISBN 0-340-58047-X

CONTENTS

6

7

8

INTRODUCTION

I love jokes, and I especially love poems
which are put together like a good joke –
verses that make me laugh.

We've got a wonderful collection of great
comic verse for you, and it's all about US –
that's me and you! – and our everyday lives.

I always feel that if you can enjoy the
funny side of things that happen in life,
then some of the less funny bits don't seem
quite so bad. Either that, or you start to be
able to find a funny side to everything.

There are some poems here that even
manage to shed a humorous light on such
very unfunny things as visits to the dentist,
coping with 'pain in the neck' brothers and
sisters or various pests at school, and
washing up or making your own bed!

A good poem can instantly conjure up a
whole situation in your mind's eye, and it
only needs a few words. Sometimes the
fewer words there are, the stronger the
image. A friend of mine passed this one on
to me. His son had heard it at school:

> We had a flower on our lawn.
> It's not there now.
> It must have gorn!

I love it. The statement of the obvious at
the end, with the mis-spelling of the word

'gorn' just to get the rhyme . . . marvellous.
It tickles my sense of humour.

I've collected a whole swag of poems that
grab me in just the same way and I've
illustrated a few where the image jumped
very clearly into my mind.

I hope you enjoy them as much as I do!

P.S. And I'd like to say a big thank-you to
Berol who supply me with all these
wonderful pens to draw with.

ALL ABOUT ME

ROLF HARRIS

Rolf Harris is great *greite* *é genial*
and an artist as well. *e um artista também* *como*
I wonder how it started *eu pergunto a min mesmo*
I just couldn't tell. *eu não consigo dizer*

dross
He draws Sylvester, Tweety Pie
and his own characters too.
If you ask him nicely
He will draw them for you.

Rolf Harris is famous
everyone knows that.
When he comes to our school
He'll be gob smacked.

Rolf Harris loves children
but soon he'll love me too.
Because when he reads this poem
He won't believe it's true.

I'm coming to the end now
I hope you've enjoyed your song
but I just want to know
Have you been to Hong Kong?

Emily Stevenson (10)

SNEAKY BILL

I'm Sneaky Bill, I'm terrible mean and
  vicious,
I steal all the cashews
  from the mixed-nuts dishes;
I eat all the icing but I won't touch the cake,
And what you won't give me,
I'll go ahead and take.

I gobble the cherries from everyone's
  drinks,
And whenever there are sausages
I grab a dozen links;
  I take both drumsticks if
  there's turkey or chicken,
  And the biggest strawberries
  are what I'm pickin';

I make sure I get the finest chop on the
  plate,
And I'll eat the portions of anyone who's
  late!

I'm always on the spot before the dinner
  bell –
I guess I'm pretty awful,
                But
                  I
                    do
                      eat
                        well!

William Cole

I'D LIKE TO BE A TEABAG

I'd like to be a teabag,
And stay at home all day –
And talk to other teabags
In a teabag sort of way . . .

I'd love to be a teabag,
And lie in a little box –
And never have to wash my face
Or change my dirty socks . . .

I'd like to be a teabag,
An Earl Grey one perhaps,
And doze all day and lie around
With Earl Grey kind of chaps.

I wouldn't have to do a thing,
No homework, jobs or chores –
Comfy in my caddy
Of teabags and their snores.

I wouldn't have to do exams,
I needn't tidy rooms,
Or sweep the floor or feed the cat
Or wash up all the spoons.

I wouldn't have to do a thing,
A life of bliss – you see . . .
Except that once in all my life

I'd make a cup of tea!

Peter Dixon

I'M GLAD I'M ME

I don't understand why everyone stares
When I take off my clothes and dance down
   the stairs.
Or when I stick carrots in both of my ears,
Then dye my hair green and go shopping at
   Sears.
I just love to dress up and do goofy things.
If I were an angel, I'd tie-dye my wings!

Why can't folks accept me the way that I
   am?
So what if I'm different and don't act like
   them?
I'm not going to change and be someone
   I'm not.
I like who I am, and I'm all that I've got!

Phil Bolsta

I LIKE TO STAY UP

I like to stay up
and listen
when big people talking
jumbie stories

I does feel
so tingly and excited
inside me

18

But when my mother say
'Girl, time for bed'

Then is when
I does feel a dread

Then is when
I does cover up
from me feet to me head

Then is when
I does wish I didn't listen
to no stupid jumbie story

Then is when
I does wish I did read
me book instead

Grace Nichols

Jumbie – Guyanese word for ghost

JUNK FOOD

Sprouts and cabbage, beans and mince
Are good for you, *they say*!
I must confess, I'd rather eat
Junk food, every day!

Fiona H. Struthers (11)

A CHILD'S LAMENT

8 pm   Please let me stay
Just 'til this last game is won.
Don't send me to bed
While I'm having such fun.

It's comfortable here
There's a great show on TV.
My eyes are wide open,
Look, can't you see?

I'm happy here,
So just for today
Don't send me to bed
Let me stay, let me stay.

8 am   Please let me stay
The night's gone so fast.
Don't make me get up
'Til my dream has passed.

It's comfortable here
And I'm not yet awake
Just five minutes more
Oh! My poor head does ache.

I'm happy here
Can't I sleep in today?
Don't make me get up
Let me stay, let me stay.

James Leggott (10)

I'M A TREBLE IN THE CHOIR

In the Choir I'm a treble
And my singing is the debbel!
I'm a treble in the Choir!
They sing high but I sing higher.
Treble singing's VERY high,
But the highest high am I!
Soon I'll burst like any bubble:
I'm a treble – that's the trouble!

Edmond Kapp

COULD HAVE BEEN WORSE

My friends have not seen London,
They've never been to France,
But yesterday at recess
They saw my underpants.

I kicked a ball, my skirt flew up
And I know what they saw.
The girls all stared and blushed and
    laughed,
The boys said, 'Oo-la-la!'

I've thought a lot about it.
This conclusion I have drawn:
I'm embarrassed that they saw them,
But I'm glad I had them on.

Bill Dodds

BIRTHDAY

It's my birthday today,
And I'm nine.
I'm having a party tonight,
And we'll play on the lawn
If it's fine.
There'll be John, Dick and Jim,
And Alan and Tim,
And Dennis and Brian and Hugh;
But the star of the show,

You'll be sorry to know,
Will be Sue.
(She's my sister, aged two,
And she'll yell till she's blue
In the face, and be sick).

My red cape is a skirt
my cousin left us last year
since she gained so much weight
she couldn't fit into it anymore.
The lacy petticoat
under my flouncy dress
is a ripped curtain
my mother was going to throw out
until I grabbed it and said,
'You never know what you can do
with stuff like that.'
My golden braid, hanging to my butt,
is a ball of wool
I was supposed to be making a cardigan
for my sister with.
She said she didn't mind waiting
a little longer.
My shepherd's staff is a golf club
with five hangers covered in pretty paper.
For shoe-buckles, I cut up some
Chinese take-away containers.
To top it all, I'm wearing my best friend's
    shower cap
with a plastic flower sticking out from the
    elastic –
how do I look?

Julia O'Callaghan

ME

My mum is on a diet,
My dad is on the booze,
My gran's out playing Bingo
And she was born to lose.

My brother's stripped his motorbike
Although it's bound to rain.
My sister's playing Elton John
Over and over again.

What a dim old family!
What a dreary lot!
Sometimes I think that I'm the only
Superstar they've got.

Kit Wright

POISONING PEOPLE IS WRONG

You've done it again haven't you?
You've eaten the cherries
And given the rest of your cake to the
     rabbit.

I SAY NOTHING.

And who gave the crust of the pork pie
To the dog?
Who?

I'll bet it was you.
He's been sick twice this morning you
  know.

ALL THE MORE REASON
FOR ME NOT TO EAT IT.

I keep finding crusts all over the house.
You're supposed to eat the whole of the
  bread
Not shove the bits you don't like in your
  pocket
And stick them in the bookcase later on.
I'd sniffed my way around
Fourteen Dickens' novels
Before I found your rotten crusts.
They'd gone green.
Are you listening?
Green, they'd gone.

SO SHE'S DESTROYED MY
PENICILLIN FACTORY.
SHE HATES SCIENTISTS.

As for that cabbage:
If you'd said you didn't want it
I wouldn't have given you so much.
You're disgusting you are.

WELL SOMETHING WAS NEEDED
TO FILL THAT GAP AT THE
BACK OF THE SOFA.

Baked potatoes
Are meant to be eaten
Not be poked about
And don't leave the skin this time:
That's the bit with all the vitamins.

**THAT'S ALSO THE BIT WITH
ALL THE MUD IF SHE'S LEFT
MY FATHER TO SCRUB THEM.**

Yes, we are having rice pudding for afters
And, yes, you do have to eat it.
In my day
You were grateful if you got rice pudding.
In my day
Things were different.

**IN HER DAY IT WAS ILLEGAL TO
POISON CHILDREN.**

Are you muttering something?

ME? NOT ME?

David Kitchen

I HATE GREENS

I hate greens!
'They're good for you,' my mother said,
'They'll make the hair curl on your head,
They'll make you grow up big and strong,
That's what your father says.' He's wrong!!

I hate greens.

Peas like bullets, beans like string,
Spinach – not like anything,
Sprouts as hard as bricks and mortar,
Slimy cabbage, slopped in water,

I hate greens.

Swamp them in tomato sauce,
Hide them in your second course,
Though they make you nearly sick,
Close your eyes and gulp them quick,

I hate greens.

Limp lettuce on a lukewarm plate,
Grit in watercress I hate,
Can't bear leeks with dirt inside,
Cauliflower with slugs that died,

I hate greens.

When we go on shopping trips,
Couldn't we have eggs and chips?
Couldn't we have chips and beans?
Don't you know what hunger means?

I HATE GREENS!!!

David King

A SLIVER OF LIVER

Just a sliver of liver they want me to eat,
It's good for my blood, they all say;
They want me to eat just the tiniest sliver
Of yukky old slimy old slithery liver;
I'm saying no thanks, not today.

No, I'll pass for tonight but tomorrow I
   might
Simply *beg* for a sliver of liver;
'Give me liver!' I'll cry. 'I'll have liver or
   die!
Oh, *please* cook me a sliver of liver!'
One piece might not do, I'll need two or a
   few,
I'll want tons of the wobbly stuff,
Of that quivery shivery livery pile
There may not be nearly enough.

Just a sliver, you say? No thanks, not today.
Tomorrow, I really can't say;
But today I would sooner eat slivers of
   glass,
Eat the tail of a skunk washed down with
   gas,
Eat slivers of sidewalks and slivers of
   swings,
Slivers and slivers of any old thing,
Than a sliver of slimy old quivery shivery
Livery liver today.

Lois Simmie

THINGS I'M NOT GOOD AT

What a shame I'm not good at making my
  bed
Or washing the dinner dishes.

What a pity I'm awful at broccoli-eating
And feeding my sister's fishes.
So sad I've no talent for cleaning my room,
All these jobs – it's so hard to get through
   them.
(If I tell you I'm no good at those kinds of
   things,
Maybe then you won't ask me to do them.)

Jeff Moss   33

MY NEW YEAR'S RESOLUTIONS

I will not throw the cat out the window
Or put a frog in my sister's bed
I will not tie my brother's shoelaces together
Nor jump from the roof of Dad's shed.
I shall remember my aunt's next birthday
And tidy my room once a week
I'll not moan at Mum's cooking (Ugh! fish
    fingers again!)
Nor give her any more of my cheek.
I will not pick my nose if I can help it
I shall fold up my clothes, comb my hair,
I will say please and thank you (even when I
    don't mean it)
And never spit or shout or even swear.
I shall write each day in my diary
Try my hardest to be helpful at school
I shall help old ladies cross the roads (even
    if they don't want to)
And when others are rude I'll stay cool.
I'll go to bed with the owls and be up with
    the larks
And close every door behind me
I shall squeeze from the bottom of every
    toothpaste tube
And stay where trouble can't find me.
I shall start again, turn over a new leaf,
Leave my bad old ways forever
Shall I start them this year, or next year
Shall I sometime, or . . . . . ?

Robert Fisher

34

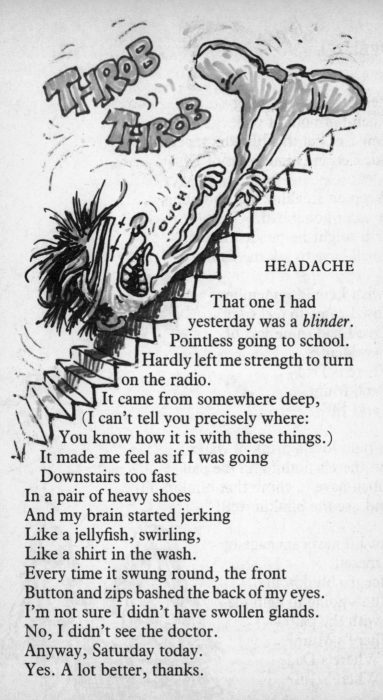

HEADACHE

That one I had
yesterday was a *blinder*.
Pointless going to school.
Hardly left me strength to turn
on the radio.
It came from somewhere deep,
(I can't tell you precisely where:
You know how it is with these things.)
It made me feel as if I was going
Downstairs too fast
In a pair of heavy shoes
And my brain started jerking
Like a jellyfish, swirling,
Like a shirt in the wash.
Every time it swung round, the front
Button and zips bashed the back of my eyes.
I'm not sure I didn't have swollen glands.
No, I didn't see the doctor.
Anyway, Saturday today.
Yes. A lot better, thanks.

Ian Whybrow

WELL ILL

I felt OK this morning
When I got out of bed.
Now I've got this blinkin paper bag
Stuck on me blinkin head.

I keep on smelling fish and chips
Or cider going bad.
Or it might be pickled onions –
I shall have to ask me dad.

I wish I could remember
How I came to feel so ill.
Have I had some sort of
   accident?
Where is Dad –
   and Mum –
   and Jill?

I would love a drink of water
But there's nothing in the pail
I shall have to climb that blinkin hill
And use the blinkin well!

But I'll never manage by
   meself
I feel so blinkin ill.
Who's going to help me
   with the pail?
Where's Mum?
   Where's Dad?
   Where's Jill?

Right! I'm goin' down the Water Board.
We're having runnin water!
I'll say me Dad'll pay for it –
They won't tumble till after!

I shall leave a little note out.
When the three of them get back
They'll get the blinkin message
Sayin, '*I'm all right now. Jack.*'

Ian Whybrow

SPOTS!

The spots say it all –
chicken-pox!

My older sister says she's got spots –
but look at me!

She says having spots is very grown up –
does this mean I get a boyfriend?

I like it here, my father a doctor,
my mum a nurse – don't want to get better,
I want to get worse!

Shaun Traynor

EAR-ACHE *(for Tym.)*

One of my tenderest memories from
   childhood
is having ear-ache; the pain was terrible
but the sympathy from Gran and mum
and head-turning dad
was immeasurable!

Gran and mum got warm butter and olive
   oil,
an eye-bowl, mixed it all together with
   cotton-wool
and placed the comforting poultice inside
   my ear-hole;

the warmth permeated my brain,
was like the hot-water bottle that warmed
   my tummy,
I slept in a cocoon of love:

they told me the doctor had come,
had felt my forehead, they paid him
with six warm eggs.

In the morning the world was cold,
the pollen-embedded ice-berg of cotton-
   wool
was hard and solidified, it drew out all the
   badness,
my forehead was chill.

I got dressed, no pain, good equilibrium,
dad said, 'this child is fit for school!'

Shaun Traynor

CHICKEN SPOTS

I've got these really itchy spots
they're climbing on my tummy
they're on my head
they're on my tail
and it isn't very funny.
They came to see me yesterday
– a few the day before
fifty on my bottom
and twenty on my jaw.

I've got a prize one on my toe
a dozen on my knee
and now they're on my thingy
– I think there's thirty-three.

I count them every evening
I give them names like Fred

Charlie Di and Daisy
Chunky Tom and Ted.

They're really awful spotties
they drive me itchy mad
the sort of itchy scratchings
I wish I never had.
Nobby's worst at itching
Lizzie's awful too
and – if you come to see me
Then I'll give a few to you . . .
   I'll give you Di and Daisy –
   I'll give you Jane and Ted
   a bucket full of itchers
   to take home to your bed . . .

You can give them to your sister
I don't care what you do
give them to a teacher
or send them to the zoo.
I don't care where you take 'em
I don't care where they go . . .
   stick them up the chimney
   or in the baby's po.
   Take them to a farmyard.
   Find a chicken pen,
   say that they're a present

      with love
      from me

         . . . to them.

Peter Dixon

MUMPS

I'm down in the dumps,
Because I've got mumps!
I hope it goes soon –
It's like a balloon!
It hurts when I yawn
And it hurts when I chew,
And sometimes I wish
That they'd change me for new!

Now **DON'T** call me fussy,
Because I am **NOT**!
I have to take tablets
And they make me hot!
I can't move around –

(That's unusual for me!)
I can't eat my breakfast,
My dinner . . . **OR** . . . tea!

I can't go to school
'cos my cheeks are so fat;
I look like a hamster –
I giggle at **THAT**!
I pull funny faces –
It helps pass the time;
I laid down and thought . . .
Then I made up this rhyme!

Nicola Jane Field (9)

LIES

When we are bored
My friend and I
Tell
Lies.

It's a competition: the prize
Is won by the one
Whose lies
Are the bigger size.

We really do:
That's true
But there isn't a prize:
That's lies.

Kit Wright

BORED

I'm ten and I'm bored
And I've nothing to do.
I'm fed up with watching
This ant on my shoe.

The Big Game has finished.
My brother won't play.
My dad says he won't let me
Watch *Match of the Day*.

I don't want to paint
Or to make model planes
Or to help Mum with cooking
Or to stroll country lanes.

I'm bored with my school,
With my books on the shelf,
And, most of all really,
Bored with being myself.

John Kitching

TEA-TIME

'When is it time for tea, mum?'
'Not yet.'
'I'll go and watch TV then.'
'OK.'
'When is it time for tea, mum?'
'Not yet.'
'I'll go to play at Billy's, then.'
'OK.'
'When is it time for tea, mum?'
'Not yet.'
'I'll go ride my bike, then.'
'OK.'
'It's tea time!'
'I'm not hungry.'

Paula Digby (11)

A CHILD OF OUR TIME
After 'I Remember' by Thomas Hood

I remember, I remember
  The block where I was born,
The high-rise horror where the
    strain
Left sleep and tempers torn.
Our flat was on the fourteenth floor,
  The shops were miles away,
And when the winter winds blew
    strong
The whole thing seemed to sway.

I remember, I remember
  The lifts were on the blink,
And Mum would often say, 'This place
  Is driving me to drink.'
There was no room to swing a cat
  And little space to grow;
I longed for neighbours when I saw
  The human ants below.

I remember, I remember
  My father's worried frown,
The night the solid concrete cracked
  And most of it fell down.
I only hoped the architect
Was living safe and sound,
The owner of a Georgian house
  And closer to the ground.

Roger Woddis

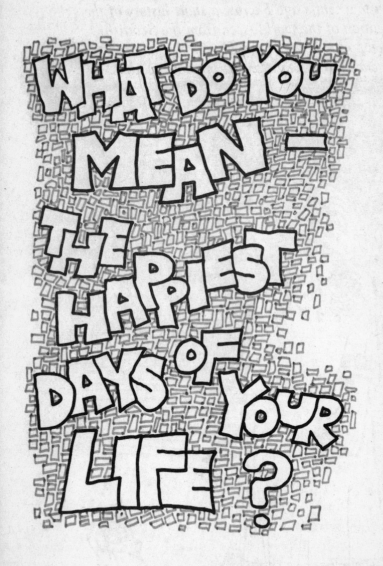

McADAM

Quite a while ago I wrote a short history of the creation of the world, seen from the Scottish viewpoint. It was based on an old, old Scottish legend that I'd written the previous week.

Do ye ken the story of the world and how it
    was created?
Did you know that Adam was a Scot?
Did ye not?
Well, on that fateful far-off day
McAdam stood and waited while the Lord
    mixed his frills and furbrillations in a pot.

And the Lord said:
'TELL ME McADAM,
HOW WOULD YOU LIKE IT?
EV'RYTHING I'M MAKING,
I MAKE FOR YOU.
ANYTHING YOU'D CARE TO NAME,
JUST TELL ME HOW YOU'D LIKE TO SEE IT,
AND I'LL CREATE IT . . .
JUST FOR YOU.
. . . . WELL?'

'Well the colour for a starter, Lord.
See everything looks grey, say,
Could you make the sky a sort of blue, for
    the noo?
Keep that lightish bluish sort of colour for
    the day,
Make the night sort of darkish blackish
    bluish,
That'll do! . . . . Phew!

'And I find it rather boring
That dull horizontal line, mind.
Mountains, hills and valleys would be good,
    if ye could.
Some whitish snow upon the peaks and

heather too that's fine.
And some tall greenish trees with, maybe,
   trunks made out of wood.
That's good.

'You're gonna need some big white woolly
   sheep
and grass for them to eat – oh –
grass should be a greenish colour too, (very
   true).
Say, white and green reminds me, could
   you make some football teams?
You could call that lot Celtic, dress the
   Rangers all in blue.
Too true Lord, too true!

'You could run some rivers down them hills
   and end 'em in a loch, Jock.
Maybe have some peat bogs over there,
   anywhere.
We'll need the water pure for when whisky
   is invented,
And the peat really filters it with extra
   special care.

'Look, have a break, Lord.
You've worked a goodly while.
Rest yourself and I will put the kettle on the
   bile.'

So Adam brewed up for the Lord
The very first cup of tea,
And sat and watched him drink it

with a smile,
Watched while he enjoyed it with a smile.

'Are ye right?
Well the break for tea is over Lord,
We'd best get back to work.
I'll suggest, and you create the gear, never
    fear.
Make porridge and some haggis and a set of
    bagpipes, too.
Tell yez what, Lord, they'll sound great for
    Hogmanay this year!'

So the work was done, the world was made.
McAdam stood surrounded by everything
    the Lord had made for him, just for him.
'NOW CAST YOUR EYES ABOUT,
DON'T LET YOUR SENSES BE
    CONFOUNDED.
IS THERE ONE, JUST A SINGLE ONE
    THING THAT I'VE FORGOT,
BEFORE I PACK IT IN . . . JIMMY?'

And McAdam said,
'Well . . . there is just one wee little thing
    that I think maybe you've
    overlooked . . .
See, I don't wish to appear ungrateful.
I would hate to have you thinking those
    thoughts of me.
Oh Lord, if you thought I was mean it
    would be hateful,
But you do owe me sixpence for the tea!'

                                    Rolf Harris

INTELLIGENCE TEST

'What do you use your eyes for?'
The white-coated man enquired.
'I use my eyes for looking,'
Said Toby, ' – unless I'm tired.'

'I see. And then you close them,'
Observed the white-coated man.
'Well done. A very good answer.
Let's try another one.

'What is your nose designed for?
What use is the thing to you?'
'I use my nose for smelling,'
Said Toby, 'Don't you, too?'

'I do indeed,' said the expert.
'That's what the thing is for.
Now I've another question to
        ask you,
Then there won't be any more.

'What are your ears intended for?
Those things at each side of your
        head?
Come on – don't be shy – I'm sure
        you can say.'
'For washing behind,' Toby said.

Vernon Scannell

BACK TO SCHOOL BLUES

Late August,
The miserable countdown starts,
Millions of kids
With lead in their hearts.
In Woolies' window: rubbers, rulers,
Geometry sets,
And a **BACK TO SCHOOL** sign –
I mean, who forgets?
In the clothes shops
Ghastly models of kids with
New satchels and blazers and shoes:
Enough to give anybody
Those Back to School Blues.

And Auntie Nell from Liverpool,
Who's down with us for a visit,
Smiles and says, 'So it's back to school
On Wednesday for you is it?
I only wish I'd got the chance
Of my schooldays over again . . .
Happiest days of my life they were –
Though I didn't realise it then . . . '
And she rabbits on like that,
Just twisting away at the screws;
She's forgotten about
The Back to School Blues.

And six and a half long weeks
Have melted away like ice cream:
That Costa Brava fortnight's
Vanished like a dream.

And Dad says, 'Look, this term
At school, could you try and do
A bit better?
For a start you could learn to spell
And write a decent letter.
And just keep away from that Hazel
    Stephens –
She's total bad news . . . '
Any wonder that I've got
Those Back to School Blues.

Eric Finney

GETTING READY FOR SCHOOL

Kate, Kate,
I know you'll be late!
Here is your satchel and here is your slate.
Don't go like that, child, your hair's in a
    state –
Kate! Kate! Kate!

Kate, Kate,
It's twenty to nine,
Take your umbrella, it may not be fine.
Oh, what a hanky – you'd better take
    mine –
Kate! Kate! Kate!

Kate, Kate,
You haven't your fare!
Here are your sandwiches on the hall chair.

What's that? – your hockey stick – where,
    darling, where?
Kate! Kate! Kate!

Kate, Kate,
Your gym shoes are here,
Won't you be needing your pencil-box,
    dear?
Try to speak slower, love, Mother can't
    hear –
Kate! Kate! Kate!

Kate, Kate,
You'd better not wait,
The two little Smith girls have just passed
    the gate.
Hurry up, darling, I know you'll be late –
Kate! Kate! Kate!

Caryl Brahms

THE HERO

Slowly with bleeding nose and aching wrists
After tremendous use of feet and fists
He rises from the dusty schoolroom floor
And limps for solace to the girl next door
Boasting of kicks and punches, cheers and
    noise,
And far worse damage done to bigger boys.

Robert Graves

STREEMIN

Im in the botom streme
Which meens Im not
   brigth
dont like reading
cant hardly write.

but all these divishns
arnt reely fair
look at the cemtery
no streemin there

Roger McGough

OUR SCHOOL

I go to Weld Park Primary,
It's near the Underpass
And five blocks past the Cemetery
And two roads past the Gas
Works with the big tower that smells so bad
   me and me mates put our hankies over our
     faces and pretend we're being attacked
       by poison gas . . . and that.

There's this playground with lines for
   rounders,
And cricket stumps chalked on the wall,
And kids with their coats for goalposts
Booting a tennis ball
Around all over the place and shoutin' and
   arguin'
   about offside and they always kick it over
     the garden wall next door and she
       goes potty and tells our head teacher
       and he gets right ratty with
         everybody and stops us playin'
         football . . .
           . . . and everything.

We have this rule at our school
You've to wait till the whistle blows
And you can't go in till you hear it
Not even if it snows
And your wellies get filled with water and
   your socks

go all soggy and start slipping down your legs
and your hands get so cold they go all
crumpled and you can't undo
the buttons of your mac when
you do get inside . . .
. . . it's true.

The best thing is our classroom.
When it's fine you can see right far,
Past the Catholic Cathedral
Right to the Morris Car
Works where me Dad works as a fitter and
sets off
right early every morning in those overalls
with his snap in his sandwich box and
a flask of tea and always moanin'
about the money . . . honest.

In Hall we pray for brotherly love
And sing hymns that are ever so long
And the Head shouts at Linda Nutter
Who's always doing wrong.
She can't keep out of trouble because
she's always talkin'
she can't stop our teacher says she
must have been injected with
a gramophone needle she talks
so much and
that made me laugh once
once
not any more though I've heard it
too often . . . teachers!

Loving your enemy sounds all right
Until you open your eyes
And you're standing next to Nolan
Who's always telling lies
About me and getting me into trouble and about
    three times a week I fight him after school
        It's like a habit I've got
            but I can't love him even though
                I screw my eyes up real hard and try like
                    mad, but if it wasn't him
                        it would be somebody else
                        I mean
            You've got to have enemies . . .
                . . . haven't you?

We sing 'O to be a pilgrim'
And think about God and heaven
And we're told the football team lost
By thirteen goals to seven
But that's not bad because St Xavier's don't
    half have
        big lads in their team and last time we played
            they beat us eighteen one and this time
                we got seven goals . . .
                    . . . didn't we?

Then we have our lessons,
We have Science and English and Maths,
Except on Wednesday morning
When our class goes to the baths
And it's not half cold and Peter Bradberry's
    fingers went all wrinkled and blue last week
        and I said, 'You're goin' to die, man'

                    but he pushed me under the water and
                    I had to
                    hold my breath
                        for fifteen minutes.
                            But he's still alive though . . .
                                . . . he is.

Friday's my favourite day though,
We have Art all afternoon
And I never care what happens
Cos I know it's home-time soon
And I'm free for two whole days but I think
    sometimes it wouldn't be half so good
        having this weekend if we didn't have five
        days
            of
                school
                    in
                        between —

Would it?

                                        Gareth Owen

THOUGHTS

All people that on Earth do dwell,
Hope Mr Foster isn't in a bad mood,
Wonder if he's here yet?
Bet he's having his breakfast,
Come ye before him and rejoice.

60

The piano's wobbly,
Might fall over,
Without our aid he did us make,
Hope Mr Foster's ill,
And for his sheep he doth us take,

O enter then his gates with praise,
Latin room's empty,
Approach with joy his courts unto,
I'm in detention today,
Have to write out 100 lines,
For it is seemly so to do.

Marcus Holburn (10)

QUESTION

Please tell me, dear Katy,
Why is it that in-
side the classroom you climb, jump and
   swing,
And somersault freely all over the floor,
The chairs and Shepperton twins.

But when we go down to
The hall for P.E.,
With ropes, horses, benches, the lot,
And masses of room to do handstands, you
   say,
'I'd rather just sit here and watch'.

Theresa Heine

We'll begin with a box, and the plural is
    boxes;
But the plural of ox should be oxen, not
    oxes.
Then one fowl is goose, but two are called
    geese;
Yet the plural of moose should never be
    meese.
You may find a lone mouse or a whole lot of
    mice,
But the plural of house is houses, not hice.
If the plural of man is always called men,
Why shouldn't the plural of pan be called
    pen?
The cow in the plural may be cows or kine,
But the plural of vow is vows, not vine.
And I speak of a foot, and you show me
    your feet,
But I give you a boot – would a pair be
    called beet?
If one is a tooth and a whole set are teeth,
Why shouldn't the plural of booth be called
    beeth?
If the singular is this, and the plural is
    these,
Should the plural of kiss be nicknamed
    kese?
Then one may be that, and three may be
    those,
Yet the plural of hat would never be hose.

SINGULAR ←→ PLURAL

SINGULAR	PLURAL
OX	OXES ?
MOOSE	MEESE
HOUSE	HICE
BOOT	BEET
KISS	KESE
HAT	HOSE
MOTHER	METHREN

We speak of a brother, and also of brethren,
But though we say mother, we never say
  methren.
The masculine pronouns are he, his, and
  him,
But imagine the feminine she, shis, and
  shim!
So our English, I think you will all agree,
Is the trickiest language you ever did see.

Anon.

JAMES HAD A MAGIC SET FOR CHRISTMAS

James had practised the tricks for days
but in front of the class
they all went wrong.
The invisible penny
dropped from his sleeve,
the secret pocket
failed to open,
his magic wand broke.
'Perhaps another time,' Miss Burroughs
    suggested,
'another day
when you've the hang of it.'

'No, Miss! Please!
I can do them, honestly.'

Suddenly
a white rabbit was sitting
on Miss Burroughs' table,
a green snake, tongue flicking,
scattered the class from the carpet,
the school was showered with golden coins
that rolled into piles on the playground.
'But, James!' Miss Burroughs said.
    'Shouldn't – '
There was a flash of lightning.

While the fire brigade coaxed
Miss Burroughs down from the oak
she'd flown into

on the other side of the playground,
the caretaker quietly swept up the mess
and Mr Pinner, the headmaster,
confiscated the magic set.
'A rather dangerous toy,' he said, 'James!'

James is still asking for it back.

Brian Morse

MATHS

I've tried counting in my head singing
    tables in my bed
Multiplying till I'm red that I'm most sure
Maths doesn't like me anymore.

Subtract and take away and minus in one day
    there isn't time to play and I'm quite sure
Maths doesn't like me anymore.

Number lines and magic squares all that
    jumping here and there
Doesn't get me anywhere
So I'm positively sure
Maths doesn't like me any more.

But for drawing I've a flair so I really
    shouldn't care but painting numbers
    that's not fair now I'm absolutely sure
Maths doesn't like me anymore.

David Woodrow (9)

SCHOOL DINNERS

If you stay to school dinners,
Better throw them aside;
A lot of kids didn't and
A lot of kids died.

The meat is made of iron,
The spuds are made of steel,
And if that don't get yer,
The afters will.

                              Anon.

MULTIPLICATION

Multiplication is vexation,
Division is as bad;
The Rule of Three it puzzles me,
And Fractions drive me mad.

Benjamin Franklin

FRUIT

Some things are true
And some are only true in school.

Like fruit. We did fruit
Today in Science. We learnt

A tomato's fruit but
A strawberry isn't.

I copied down the diagrams
And all the notes –

'Cos I knew I had to
Pretend it was true

I'm not daft, I know when
To make believe:

That's why I'm
Set One for Science.

Mick Gowar

One day Miss Twiss
the primary teacher
turned into a fish
and began to lecture

to her children dear
holding the chalk
in her fish's tail.
As she couldn't walk

she stood up straight
as a snake might do
and her scales were white
and sometimes blue.

'I'll tell you a tail,'
she told the boys
and seemed surprised
when they made a noise.

'I'll teach you the scales,'
she told the girls
and seemed surprised
at their subsequent twirls.

'I'll teach you to skate,'
she said with a grin
and seemed surprised
at the noise and the din.

When the cat came in
she slid away
and has never been heard of
till this day.

Iain Crichton Smith

DOBBO'S FIRST SWIMMING LESSON

Dobbo's fists
spiked me to the playground wall
nailed me to the railings.

The plastic ball
he kicked against my skinny legs
on winter playtimes

Bounced a stinging red-hot bruise
across the icy tarmac.

The day we started swimming
we all jumped in
laughed and splashed, sank beneath
the funny tasting water.

Shivering in a corner
Dobbo crouched, stuck to the side
sobbing like my baby brother
when all the lights go out.

David Harmer

NEW BOY'S VIEW OF RUGGER

When first I played I nearly died.
   The bitter memory still rankles –
They formed a scrum with *me* inside!
   Some kicked the ball and some my
   ankles.
I did not like the game at all,
   Yet, after all the harm they'd done me,
Whenever I came near the ball
   They knocked me down and stood upon
   me.

Rupert Brooke

Playing for the School today;
Ten minutes to the start of play;
Run out on the football ground,
Kick the practice ball around.

Time now for the Captains' call;
We take the kick, I've got the ball.
Fool that winger. Spring on ahead,
Draw two defence and pass to Ted.

He foot-traps. Holds. I've marked a space;
Ted flicks to Nick; I start to race;
Nick slides a low one to my feet.
Here comes the back. Just him to beat.

Watch the goalie, let the ball roll;
He runs forward. Shoot! It's a goal!
No it isn't. I'm sick in bed.
'Up tomorrow,' the Doctor said.

To make things worse. Great spots of rain
Spatter over the window pane.
Rain! That's no little April shower.
Been roaring down now, half an hour.

I hear the phone ring in the hall
And Mum's voice saying, 'I'll tell Paul.'
'A flooded pitch. Fit for a duck.'
(Poor chaps, that really is bad luck.)

A flooded pitch! No chance of play!
The Match put off a week today!
I should be fit then for the Team.
Perhaps I'll score, as in my dream!

Robert Sparrow

ONE OF OUR RUBBERS IS MISSING

Ladies and gentlemen,
one of our rubbers is missing,
a blue pencil rubber
used twice or thrice
before morning break
and never seen again.

Now this class has a very good record,
only two 10ps and an anorak
disappeared in mysterious circumstances
in a term and a half.
Search your consciences, check your
    pockets.

No result? A shame.
I was hoping not to have to use
my Sherlock Holmes act
so early in the week.
I suppose I better look for suspects
before I begin turning out coat linings.

Ah, a development! Nicola thinks
she saw the rubber
after play after all.

Well, she is the expert –
it was hers.
Where was it, Nicola?
Come on! No need to be shy.
You lent it to Richard.
What has Richard to say?
She didn't. Didn't what?
Oh, didn't lend it.

Ladies and gentlemen,
this is turning into
one of the most difficult cases
this teacher-detective has ever dealt with.
Quiet a moment! Who shouted out that
Nicola never had the rubber in the first
    place?
Ah, Kerry. You. Stand up a moment.
An interesting theory.
What's that, Lisa?
Silence a moment.
Ah, Kerry has a blue rubber
in her desk too? She has?
May we see it?
Thank you, Kerry. I see,
a blue Mickey Mouse rubber,
just like yours, Nicola.
Well, Kerry, it's very well preserved
if Father Christmas gave you it
two months ago.

I see. Your mother wouldn't let you
bring it to school till today.
Very wise of her I might say.

Now, Kerry, there's no reason to cry.
No one's accusing you of anything
yet. Yes
I'm quite sure your dad will back you up.
And there's no reason for you to cry,
   Nicola,
either. I think it ought to be me crying.
In fact I think I am.
Am what? Crying!

Now listen, Kerry,
isn't there the faintest chance
you left your immaculate rubber
at home?
None.
Well that's pretty definite.
Now what about you, Nicola?
Might you by any chance . . .
No.
Richard, you're trying to say something.
What's that?

Richard, let's get this clear.
Nicola lent you the rubber
and you lent the rubber to Kerry
who said she was going to keep it
and would bash you up if you let on –
duff you over – it's more or less the same
   thing.
Sorry, Hayley, dear – what did you say?
That you saw Kerry bring the rubber
to school this morning.
You're quite sure?

No honestly,
there's no reason to fetch the class Bible.

KNOCK KNOCK KNOCK
Yes, do come in.
Oh, hello, headmaster.
No, no trouble at all.
Just bashing my head against a brick wall.

Brian Morse

MY TEACHER

What's wrong with my teacher?
Does he shout too
                    much?
Does he give you too much
                    homework?
Does he keep you in too
                    long?
Does he actually like
                    you?
Suddenly it dawned
    on me,
        He
            picks
                his
                    nose.

*Deepak
Kalha*

THE LESSON

A poem that raises the question:
Should there be capital punishment in schools?

Chaos ruled OK in the classroom
as bravely the teacher walked in
the nooligans ignored him
his voice was lost in the din

'The theme for today is violence
and homework will be set
I'm going to teach you a lesson
one that you'll never forget'

He picked on a boy who was shouting
and throttled him then and there
then garotted the girl behind him
(the one with grotty hair)

Then sword in hand he hacked his way
between the chattering rows
'First come, first severed' he declared
'fingers, feet, or toes'

He threw the sword at a latecomer
it struck with deadly aim
then pulling out a shotgun
he continued with his game

The first blast cleared the backrow
(where those who skive hang out)
they collapsed like rubber dinghies
when the plug's pulled out

'Please may I leave the room sir?'
a trembling vandal enquired
'Of course you may' said teacher
put the gun to his temple and fired

The Head popped a head round the
    doorway
to see why a din was being made
nodded understandingly
then tossed in a grenade

And when the ammo was well spent
with blood on every chair
Silence shuffled forward
with its hands up in the air

The teacher surveyed the carnage
the dying and the dead
He waggled a finger severely
'Now let that be a lesson' he said

Roger McGough

CONVERSATIONS

Sitting in class,
listening to
conversations.
Eddy and Frog
playing cards,
'I never put that down.'
'Yes you did.'

'Shame,' says Alrick.

Kevin P. casually
beating up
Kevin B.
'Get off,'
'Shut your gob.'

Butts and Byron
doing their work,
for once,
'What about number seven?'
'Me no know.'

Tina and the two Lesleys,
talking,
'She went out last night.'
'You never believe who I saw yesterday.'

Nisha, Nayyar and Sumathi
listen to
Jackie and Claudia
arguing,

'Stop writing on my book!'
'Bloody well leave off!'

Errol points out
the window,
Dapo answers him,
'Fisk.'
'Shame.'

Tracey, Janet and Gaby
talk amongst themselves,
loudly,
'Have you done your homework?'
'Staying dinners?'

Sir stands up
'4i please be quiet!'
Mr Munro is now in
tears.

Marie and Pauline
writing,
on the desk,
'Did you see that film last night?'
'We've got French.'

Ashok and Ramji,
quiet.

Gary, Dean and Lee,
fighting,
'Stop strangling me!'
'You git.'

'I wonder why sir's got his head on the
    desk?'

Deepak Kalha

OUR TEACHER'S VOICE

Our teacher lost his voice today.
We said we'd look for it,
poking into cupboards
and under tables till he croaked:

SQUEAK

'Will you stop all this silliness
and go and get on with your work.'

'Have you really lost your voice?'
we asked, till someone tried
the same daft question once
too often, and he slapped down
a metre rule so hard that it broke.

Then he wrote what we had to do
on the board, we pretended
we didn't understand, then laughed
as he tried to explain,
voice reduced to whispering,
eyes darting this way and that.

At three thirty we bundled off home.
'Our teacher lost his voice today,'
we called out, to anyone who'd listen.

'I'm not surprised,' Mum said,
'That must have been rotten,
knowing you lot!'

'What do you mean, knowing us lot?' we
   said,
'He yells too much,
he wore it out!'

But if he's not there tomorrow,
the Head might take our class
and he's been known to cuff and clout.
Let's hope our teacher's voice
is back to a shout.

Brian Moses   83

WHEN I TELEPHONED THE SCHOOL SOMEONE SAID . . .

Michelle's got the measles,
Matthew's got the mumps.
Richard says his throat's on fire,
And Jane's nose is out in lumps.

Simon has the jitters,
Susan has the shakes,
Wendy broke her forearm
Doing wheelies on her skates.

Nigel smashed his finger
Hammering nails in bits of wood,
Karen's got 'Artist's Tummy',
(Brian put paint in her food!)

Bouncing on the single bed
David broke six teeth,
His sister Kim is flat as a pancake –
She shouldn't have slept underneath!

Jeremy's nose is purple
His hands and feet are blue;
Shivering there in pyjamas –
Locked himself in the loo!

So there's no-one here but us teachers
So please phone back tonight,
The kids are all off with sickness

And The **HEAD** has just turned white.

John Rice

'But then, as our old P.E. master, Wally,
used to say – '
Wally? Wally? Old P.E. master?
I re-found the station
and tuned it in.

'Why! I know that speaker!' I said. 'I'm
    sure of it.'
'Give me the *Radio Times*.
Yes, someone I went to school with,
David Hennessy. He was the year above me.
That's my old games master he's talking
    about!'

How it comes back! Wally!
How it comes back!
A tall hard-eyed middle-aged
whistle-swinging-on-a-cord bully
with a cropped head of hair

and a false public-school accent
underlaid with indelible cockney.
How he ruined my first and second year
Tuesdays and Thursdays!
How it comes back – the bully!

An ex-international rugby referee
even the sportsmen among us hated,
a permanent crêpe bandage on his knee-cap,
like a badge of status –
or a target.

In the second year a lad from Halesowen
deliberately head-butted the knee
during a game of pirates.
How he hopped! How he tried not to
    scream!
Wally never troubled him again.

'But you were eleven then, twelve,'
my wife says. 'You can't bear grudges that
    long.'
'Look,' I say. 'I'm sweating even now.
Feel my hands if you don't believe me.'

I thought of writing to Hennessy,
inviting him for a drink if he was ever in
    Birmingham.
But he'd mentioned Wally too kindly,
as if – somehow – he'd managed to get the
    man's measure.
No, I thought. We'd have nothing in
    common.
Nothing at all.

Brian Morse

OH BRING BACK HIGHER STANDARDS

Oh bring back higher standards –
the pencil and the cane –
if we want education then we must have
    some pain.
Oh, bring us back all the gone days
Yes, bring back all the past . . .

let's put them all in rows again – so we can
   see who's last.
Let's label all the good ones
(the ones like you and me)
and make them into prefects – like prefects
   used to be.
We'll put them on the honours board
. . . as honours ought to be,
and write their names in burnished script –
for all the world to see.
We'll have them back in uniform,
we'll have them doff their caps,
and learn what manners really are
. . . for decent kind of chaps!
. . . So let's label all the good ones,
we'll call them 'A's and 'B's –
and we'll parcel up the useless ones
and call them 'C's and 'D's.
. . . We'll even have an 'E' lot!
. . . and 'F' or 'G' maybe!!
. . . so they can know they're useless,
. . . and not as good as me.

For we've got to have the stupid –
And we've got to have the poor
Because –
              if we don't have them . . .
              well . . . what are prefects for?

Peter Dixon

THE SCHOOL CARETAKER

In the corner of the playground
Down dark and slimy stairs,
Lived a Monster with a big nose
Full of curly hairs.

He had a bunch of keyrings
Carved out of little boys,
He confiscated comics
And all our favourite toys.

He wore a greasy uniform,
Looked like an undertaker,
More scary than a horror film,
He was the school caretaker.

I left the school some years ago;
Saw him again the other day,
He looked rather sad and old
Shuffling on his way.

It's funny when you grow up
How grown-ups start growing down,
And the snarls upon their faces
Are no more than a frown.

In the corner of the playground
Down dark and slimy stairs,
Sits a lonely little man
With a nose full of curly hairs.

Brian Patten

A TEACHER'S LAMENT

Don't tell me the cat ate your math sheet,
And your spelling words went down the
   drain,
And you couldn't decipher your homework,
Because it was soaked in the rain.

Don't tell me you slaved for hours
On the project that's due today,
And you would have had it finished
If your snake hadn't run away.

Don't tell me you lost your eraser,
And your worksheets and pencils, too,
And your papers are stuck together
With a great big glob of glue.

I'm tired of all your excuses;
They are really a terrible bore.
Besides, I forgot my own work,
At home in my study drawer.

Kalli Dakos

WHAT, MISS?

Homework?
Did we have homework?

You was away on Monday, miss,
So we thought you'd be away today.

I've done it, miss,
But I've left my book up my nan's.

I lent my book to Darren
And he's away today.

I've got my book, miss,
But I did the work on paper
And I think I left it at home.

My baby sister
Got hold of all my books
And was sick on them.

I thought I had a dental appointment
This morning, miss,
But it's this afternoon
So I've got the books for this afternoon
When I'll be at the dentist
But I haven't got this morning's books
Because I thought I wan't here.

I had a brain relapse, miss.

David Kitchen

TELEPHONING TEACHER

Teacher! Teacher!
I'm having trouble with my story!
It starts quite well,
But the ending's gory.
Teacher! Teacher!

I'm having trouble with my sums!
I'm running out of fingers,
I'm running out of thumbs!
Teacher! Teacher!
I'm having trouble with P.E.!
I've a crick in my shoulder,
A pain in my knee!
Teacher! Teacher!
I feel a proper fool!
Teacher! Teacher!
I don't like school!
Teacher! Teacher!
I can't come today!
I'll get my mum to write a note,
So I can stop away.
Teacher! Teacher!
Don't be cross,
Teacher! Teacher!
I don't give a toss.
I don't go at all for this
    learning lark,
I'd rather go and wag it in
    the park.
Teacher! Teacher!
It's no use!
I'll think up
A marvellous excuse.
My eyes are crossed,
And my legs are lead,
And I'm going to stay,
All day,
In bed.

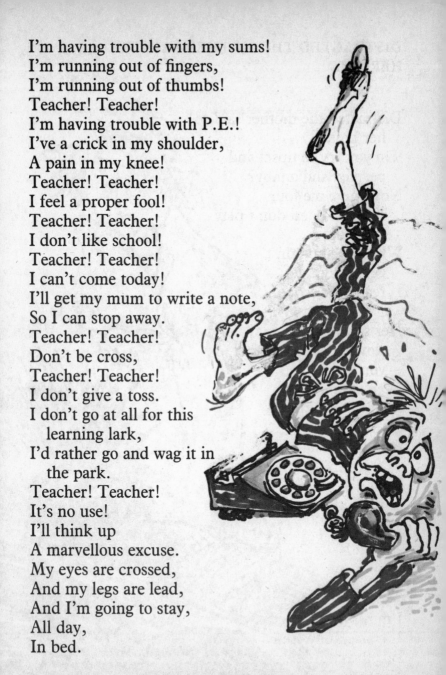

John Cunliffe

DISTRACTED THE MOTHER SAID TO HER BOY

Distracted the mother said to
    her boy,
'Do you try to upset and
    perplex and annoy?
Now, give me four
    reasons – and don't play
    the fool –
Why you shouldn't
    get up and get
    ready for school.'

Her son replied
    slowly, 'Well, mother,
    you see,
I can't stand the
teachers and they
detest me;
And there isn't a boy
or a girl in the place
That I like or,
in turn, that delights
in my face.'

'And I'll give you two reasons,' she said,
    'why you ought
Get yourself off to school before you get
    caught;
Because, first, you are forty, and, next, you
    young fool,
It's your job to be there.
You're the head of the
    school.'

Gregory Harrison

LATE COMERS

There's a special club
In our school;
The late-comers club.

They catch slow buses
From distant places,
Never have alarm-clocks,
Always have excuses,
Wonderful excuses!

In assembly,
They sit in a bunch,
Just inside the door,
Pretending not to exist.

They grow up to be;
Glib of tongue,
Never, seemingly, in the wrong;
Novelists;
Television script-writers;
Antique dealers;
Politicians.

Such are the benefits,
Of creative excuse-making.

John Cunliffe

A STUDENT'S PRAYER

Now I lay me down to rest,
I pray I pass tomorrow's test.
If I should die before I wake,
That's one less test I'll have to take.

Anon.

I WAS MUCKING ABOUT IN CLASS

I was mucking about in class

Mr Brown said,
Get out and take your chair with me
I suppose he *meant* to say
Take your chair with you
so Dave said,
Yeah – you heard what he said
        get out and take my chair with him
so Ken said,
Yeah – get out and take his chair with me
so I said to Mr Brown
Yessir – shall I take our chair with you, sir?

Wow
That meant **BIG TROUBLE**

Michael Rosen

I LOVE TO DO MY HOMEWORK

I love to do my homework,
It makes me feel so good.
I love to do exactly
As my teacher says I should.

I love to do my homework,
I never miss a day.
I even love the men in white
Who are taking me away.

Anon.

The bells ring loud; the doors swing wide,
And out storm pupils; the raging tide
Of pigtails, freckles, old school ties,
Crisp blue shirts and new black eyes,
Pendants, rings, and snapped shoe laces,
Grubby knees and impish faces,
Streaming down the long dark halls,
Clutching bags and soccer balls.

The teachers follow, tired and weary,
In wrinkled shirts and suits of dreary
Greys and browns and pin-striped blues,
Loosened ties and polished shoes,
Exhausted from another day
Of horror pupils with tricky ways,
Who prank and jest and chance their arm,
To annoy the 'Teach', then dance from
    harm.

They struggle past the staff-room door,
A forbidden pass of ancient lore,
And grab a cup of sacred drink
And down it straight then start to think
Of how to gain a sweet revenge
Upon the kids and start to mend
Their evil ways of tricks and jokes,
Who delight in having fun to poke

And then they turn unto the dread
Of marking homework in pain unsaid,
Punctuation, spelling errors,

The bungling of the tiny terrors,
Little swines who've done it wrong,
Wrong page, wrong number, wrong ALL
  DAY LONG!
Whose repeated blunders make them groan,
Oh, they dread to take the homework
  home!

And while all this is going on
The pupils make a beeline home,
And laugh and smirk and scream with joy
(The girls as well, not just the boys).
This war, it shall go on and on
Unceasing, it lasts for all time long
Us versus Them, the simple way
To summarize each new school day.

Scott R. Paterson (14)

PLAYING TRUANT

Davy
was no fan
of the School Attendance man

Maybe
canes and schools
aren't really suitable for fools

the Law
still demanded
that school should be attended

what's more
the Headmaster
proclaimed him a disaster

being no
great bookworm
his liking for lessons was lukewarm

even so he was fluent
in the art of playing truant

Raymond Wilson

THE REBEL CHILD

Most days when I
Go off to school
I'm perfectly contented
To follow the rule.

Enjoy my history,
My music, my sums,
Feel a little sorry
When home time comes.

But on blowabout mornings
When clouds are wild
And the weather in a tumult –
I'm a rebel child.

I sit quite calmly,
My face at rest,
Seem quite peaceable,
Behave my best;

But deep inside me
I'm wild as a cloud,
Glad the sky is thrown about
Glad the storm's loud!

And when school's over
And I'm out at last,
I'll laugh in the rain,
Hold my face to the blast.

Be free as the weather,
Bellow and shout
As I run through all the puddles –
'School's out! School's out!'

Leslie Norris

DUNCE

At school I never gained a prize,
Proving myself the model ass;
Yet how I watched with wistful eyes,
And cheered my mates who topped the
    class.
No envy in my heart I found,
Yet none was worthier to own
Those precious books in vellum bound,
Than I, a dreamer and a drone.

No prize at school I ever gained
(Shirking my studies, I suppose):
Yes, I remember being caned
For lack of love of Latin prose.
For algebra I won no praise,
In grammar I was far from bright:
Yet, oh, how Poetry would raise
In me a rapture of delight!

I never gained a prize at school;
The dullard's cap adorned my head;
My masters wrote me down a fool,
And yet – I'm sorry they are dead.
I'd like to go to them and say:
'Yours is indeed a tricky trade.
My honoured classmates, where are they?
Yet I, the dunce, brave books have made.'

Oh, I am old and worn and grey,
And maybe have not long to live;
Yet 'tis my hope at some Prize Day
At my old school the Head will give
A tome or two of mine to crown
Some pupil's well-deserved success –
Proving a scapegrace and a clown
May win at last to worthiness.

Robert Service

DOWN BY THE SCHOOL GATE

There goes the bell
it's half past three
and down by the school gate
you will see . . .

. . . ten mums in coats, talking
    nine babes in prams, squawking
    eight dads their cars parking
    seven dogs on leads barking

    six toddlers all squabbling
    five Grans on bikes wobbling
    four child-minders running
    three bus drivers sunning

    two teenagers dating
    one lollipop man waiting . . .

The school is out,
it's half past three
and the first to the school gate
. . . is me!

Wes Magee

SCHOOL REPORT

'*Too easily satisfied. Spelling still poor.
  Her grammar's erratic. Lacks care.
Would succeed if she worked. Inclined to be
  smug.*'
I think that's a wee bit unfare.

Ah well, their it is! Disappointing perhaps,
  For a mum what has always had brane,
But we can't all have looks or be good at our
  books . . .
  She's her father all over agane.

Carole Paine

Dear Sir,
This may sound like an excuse –
for which I apologize –
but I did not realize that today's exam
was English Lit
and therefore revised my physics last night
after the late film –
though not for more than ten minutes
should you worry I wasted my time.
In any case Denise Levertov borrowed
all my English Lit books last summer
and has not yet returned them
so even if I had not been so sleepy
it would have been precious little use
and frustrating
if I had tried my best to no avail.
Last night's film was okay
and called *The Prince of Darkness*.
Even though it was in black and white
and the sound was crackly
I enjoyed it. This prince,
whose name was Hamlet, pretends
to go mad and kills his girlfriend's dad
by poking a sword through a curtain.
Sometimes I wouldn't mind getting
my girlfriend's dad behind a curtain
and sticking a sword in him
especially when he says you're both only
    thirteen
and a late-night as far as you're concerned
is a quarter past nine – got it, chuck?

This Prince was a really mixed-up person.
If I'd behaved like him
my mum and the headmaster
would have had me
straight down the cop-shop within five
    seconds
but luckily for him he lived in History,
not to mention being an aristocrat.
Funny – he talked to himself a lot,
just like the fellow in that Shakespeare
you tried to make us read last term.
Anyway, sorry again,
I see that half the class have left already.
Mr Pankhurst doesn't seem able to stop
    them.

Ciao, sir. Yours faithfully, Terry Atkins

Brian Morse

JUST MESSIN' ABOUT

THE LEADER

I wanna be the leader
I wanna be the leader
Can I be the leader?
Can I? I can?
Promise? Promise?
Yippee, I'm the leader
I'm the leader

OK what shall we do?

Roger McGough

THE BARKDAY PARTY

For my dog's birthday party
I dressed like a bear.
My friends came as lions
and tigers and wolves and
    monkeys.
At first, Runabout couldn't believe
the bear was really me. But
he became his old self again
when I fitted on his magician's
    top hat.
Runabout became the star, running
    about jumping up on chairs
    and tables barking at every
    question asked him.
Then, in their ordinary clothes,

my friend Brian and his dad arrived
with their boxer, Skip. And with us
knowing nothing about it, Brian's dad
mixed the dog's party meat and milk
with wine he brought. We started
singing. Runabout started to yelp.
All the other six dogs joined –
yelping
   Happy Barkday to you
     Happy Barkday to you
   Happy Barkday Runabout
     Happy Barkday to you!

                   James Berry

THE COMMENTATOR

Good afternoon and welcome,
This is Danny Markey your commentator
Welcoming you to this international
Between England and Holland,
Which is being played here this afternoon
At four Florence Terrace.
And the pitch looks in superb condition
As Danny Markey prepares
To kick off for England;
And this capacity crowd roars
As Markey, the England captain,
Puts England on the attack.
Straight away it's Markey
With a lovely pass to Keegan,
Keegan back to Markey,

Markey in possession now
Jinking skilfully past the dustbin
And a neat flick inside the cat there,
What a brilliant player this Markey is
And still only nine years old!
Markey to Francis,
Francis to Markey,
Markey is through . . .
No, he's been tackled by the drainpipe;
But he's won the ball back brilliantly
And he's advancing on the Dutch keeper
     now,
It must be a goal,
He comes off his line
But Markey chips him brilliantly
It's a goal . . .
No.
It's gone into Mrs Spence's next door.
And Markey's going round
To ask for his ball back.
The Crowd is silent now.
If he can't get the ball back
It could be the end of this international.
And now the door's opening
And yes, it's Mrs Spence,
Mrs Spence has come to the door,
And wait a minute, she's shaking her head,
She is shaking her head,
She is not going to let Markey
Have his ball back.
What is the referee going to do?
Markey looks very dejected here,
He's walking back, hanging his head . . .

What's he doing now?
He seems to be waiting
And my goodness me
He's going back,
Markey is going back for the ball,
What a brilliant and exciting move;
He waited until the front door was closed
And then went back for that lost ball.
He's searching now,
He's searching for that ball
Down there by the compost heap
And wait a minute,
He's found it!
He's found that ball
And that's marvellous news
For the hundred thousand fans gathered
    here,
Who are showing their appreciation
In no uncertain fashion.
But wait a minute,
The door's opening once more;
It's her, it's Mrs Spence!
And she's waving her fist
And shouting something
But I can't make out what it is.
She's obviously not pleased.
And Markey's off,
He's running round in circles
Dodging this way and that
With Mrs Spence in hot pursuit,
And he's past her,
What skills this boy has.
But Mr Spence is here too

And Bruce their dog,
Markey is going to have to
Pull out something extra
To get out of this one;
He's only got Mr Spence and the bassett
To beat now. He's running straight at him.
And he's down, he's down on all fours;
What is he doing?
And Oh my goodness
That is brilliant,
That is absolutely brilliant,
He's gone between Spence's legs.
But he's got him,
This rugged tackler has got him,
He's got him by the jacket,
And Bruce is in there too,
Bruce has him by the seat of the pants,
He'll never get out of this one.
But he has,
He has got away;
He wriggled out of his jacket
And left part of his trousers with Bruce;
This boy is absolute dynamite.
He's over the wall, he's clear,
They'll never catch him now,
He's on his bike and
Through the front gate
And I don't think we'll see any more of
    Markey
Till the coast's clear
And it's safe to come home;
So this is Danny Markey . . .
Handing you back to the studio.

Gareth Owen

DOWN TO EARTH

I climbed a tree,
I got too high,
My dad said I could
Touch the sky.

But I fell down,
And bumped my head.
So I think I'll stick
To the ground instead.

Tony Bradman

'Third grade Chinese women, next please!'
We came shuffling out of the stage wings,
squinting at the footlights, holding
   umbrellas,
Mrs Fox arranged us by tugging our arms;
then she'd point to the pianist dramatically
and say, 'From the top, Mrs Henderson,
if you please', and start to dance.
'Remember you're Chinese, O.K.?
They aren't clod-hoppers in China,
so when you make your entrance
I want little teensy steps, like so.'
She bowed her head, holding her umbrella
up high and tip-toed in.
'Now, when Mrs Henderson hits these
   chords,
hold your umbrellas in front of you
and twirl two-three-four, five-six-seven-
   eight.
Then step-curtsy, step-curtsy,
shuffle-step, shuffle-step, to the right:
twirl two-three-four, to the left: two-three-
   four.
This is where we come to the tricky part.

Julia O'Callaghan

CAROLLING AROUND THE ESTATE

The six of us met at Alan's house
  and Jane brought a carol sheet
that she got free from the butcher's shop
  when she bought the Sunday meat.

Jeremy had a new lantern light
  made by his Uncle Ted
and Jim had 'borrowed' his Dad's new torch
  which flashed white, green, and red.

Our first call was at Stew Foster's place
  where we sang 'Three Kings' real well.
But his Mother couldn't stand the row
  and she really gave us hell!

We drifted on from door to door
  singing carols by lantern light.
Jane's lips were purple with the cold;
  my fingers were turning white.

Around nine we reached the chippie shop
  where we ordered pies and peas,
and with hot grease running down our
  hands
  we started to defreeze.

I reached home tired out, but my Mum said,
  'Your cousin Anne's been here.
She's carolling tomorrow night
  and I said you'd go, my dear.'

Wes Magee

COME ON IN THE WATER'S LOVELY

Come on in the water's lovely
It isn't really cold at all
Of course you'll be quite safe up this end
If you hold tight to the wall.

Of course that fat boy there won't drown
   you
He's too busy drowning Gail
Just imagine you're a tadpole.
I *know* you haven't got a tail.

Oh come on in the water's lovely
Warm and clear as anything
All the bottom tiles are squiggly
And your legs like wriggly string.

Come on in the water's lovely
It's no good freezing on the side
How do you know you're going to drown
Unless you've really tried.

What? You're really going to do it?
You'll jump in on the count of three?
Of course the chlorine doesn't blind you
Dive straight in and you'll soon see.

One – it isn't really deep at all.
Two – see just comes to my chin.
Three – oh there's the bell for closing time
And just as you jumped in!

Gareth Owen

116

COWBOY

I remember, on a long,
Hot, summer, thirsty afternoon
Hiding behind a rock
With Wyatt Earp
(His glasses fastened on with sellotape)

The Sioux were massing for their last attack

We knew

No 7th Cavalry for us
No bugles blaring in the afternoon
I held my lone star pistol in my hand
Thinking
I was just seven and too young to die
Thinking
Save the last cap
For yourself.

Richard Hill

CHILDREN AT LARGE

... is mam.
... is gran.
... d U.

He still had the toothache.
   EEEGH!
'Ulie's making noises!' said Jason.
'Ulie's pulling faces!' said Alice.
'So would *you*!' said U.

When Ulie got back home
He was trying not to cry.
   O-O-OH!
'To the dentist!' said his mam.
'Told you so!' said his gran.
'Oh, leave off!' said U.

When Ulie sat in the chair
He felt the dentist's probe.
   GARRGH!
'Do sit still!' said the nurse.
'This won't hurt!' said the dentist.
'Who're you kidding?' said U.

When Ulie saw the drill
He bit the dentist's hand.
   SCREECH!

'You need a smack!' said the nurse.
'Your teeth will rot!' said the dentist.
'I don't care!' said U.

When Ulie felt the needle
He suddenly went numb.
   AH-HUM!
'Open wide!' said the dentist.
'All over now!' said the nurse.
'Nothing to it!' said U.

Jennifer Curry

THOUGHTS FROM A DENTIST'S
WAITING ROOM

Please let there be a powercut.
        Just a tiny little one.
Just before he gets the drill near my
                mouth.

One down, two to go

Or maybe he'll be struck down,
By a hitherto undiscovered and as yet
            incurable palsy
which only lasts for the ten minutes I'm
with him, and then vanishes forever?

Two down, one to go

Maybe he got the notes mixed up.

'Ridiculous,' he'll say, 'You don't need
fillings at all!'
'They're old Mrs Crabtree's notes!' (even
though she has dentures).

NEXT PLEASE!

Why is the dentist the
only one who is
ever smiling?

Amanda Evans (14)

WHOPPERS

'I'm having a pony for Christmas,
And a meal at a posh hotel.'
'That's nothing, I'm having video,
And two colour tellies as well.'

'My dad's having a Rolls Royce car.'
'Well, my dad's having two –
One for his window-cleaning gear
And one for mum – brand new.'

'My mum's having a baby.'
'Well, my mum's having twins –
Or maybe she'll have triplets,
Or even quads or quins.'

'I'm having a sailing dinghy:
Cor, won't the neighbours go green!'
'We're having the yacht Britannia
Bought secondhand from the Queen.'

'We're off to the Costa Brava,
Dad's getting tickets quite soon.'
'I'll think of you then while we're on
Our luxury tour of the moon.'

. . . . .

'To tell you the truth, I've been fibbing
And boasting, I realize.'
'That's nothing: I've not been telling fibs,
But monstrous, walloping lies!'

Eric Finney

JOHNNY

Johnny used to find content
In standing always rather bent,
Like an inverted
    letter J.
  His angry relatives
    would say,
'Stand up!
  don't slouch!
You've got a spine,

Stand like a lamppost,
  not a vine!'
One day they heard an
  awful crack –
He'd stood up straight –
  it broke his back!

Emma Rounds

GLORIA

Gloria was perfect
In lots of little ways.
She had at least a million friends
And always got straight As.
I think she was the cutest girl
That I have ever met;
The apple of her mother's eye
And every teacher's pet.

But then one day it happened.
The unthinkable, to wit:
Gloria the Perfect
Got a king-sized zit!
Big and red and puffy,
It covered half her brow.
Funny thing about it, though –
I like her better now.

Joyce Armor

THE OUTLAW

Into the house of a Mrs MacGruder
Came a very big outlaw
With a real six-shooter,
And he kicked the door
With his cowboy boot
And he searched the place
For valuable loot,
And he didn't take off his cowboy hat
But he quickly unlimbered his cowboy gat
And he cocked the gun
And he took his aim
And he called that Mrs MacG by name
And he said in a terrible outlaw drawl,
'Git me that cake . . . and git it all!'

And Mrs MacGruder patted his head,
'You may have a slice with some milk,' she
    said.

Felice Holman

GROWING UP

I know a lad called Billy
Who goes along with me
He plays this game
Where he uses my name
And makes people think that he's me.

Don't ever mess with Billy
He's a vicious sort of bloke
He'll give you a clout
For saying nowt
And thump you for a joke.

My family can't stand Billy
Can't bear him around the place
He won't eat his food
He's always rude
And wears scowls all over his face.

No one can ever break Billy
He's got this look in his eye
That seems to say
You can whale me all day
But you'll not make Billy cry.

He has a crazy face has Billy
Eyes that look but can't see
A mouth like a latch
Ears that don't match
And a space where his brains should be.

Mad Billy left one morning
Crept away without being seen
Left his body for me
That fits perfectly
And a calm where his madness had been.

Gareth Owen

I carry my friends like a crew on a ship.
They say they're all there; that no-one's
   been missed.
They have all signed their names in
   coloured felt-tip,
Over my plaster, from elbow to wrist.

There's Denis and Geoffrey and Arthur and
   Wayne,
Andrew and Henry, and new Carolyn;
And Josephine, Alice and Mary and Jane,
Peter, and Paul, his identical twin.

And Freda and Laurence and Tony and
  Nell,
Robert and Rachel, and Alan and Tim;
'Brains' Alexander, and his sister Michelle.
(She can play football much better than
  him.)

My sister has printed I, L, E, E, N.
She's only five so her spelling's not good.
Here's Willoughby, (Honest!) Edward and
  Ben,
And once again: – Wayne; Of course, but *he*
  would.

I've just found a name that I don't really
  know.
A girl? Or a boy? Find out if I can.
Who was the person who wrote 'J' and 'O'?
'Your best mate. Who else? It's me,
  Jonathan.

The others all wrote and left only one space.
Now you're my best friend. Don't mean any
  harm.
But bags I to write in the very first place,
The next time you think of breaking your
  arm.'

                              Robert Sparrow

IT'S DARK IN HERE

I am writing these lines
From inside a lion,
And it's rather dark in here.
So please excuse the handwriting
Which may not be too clear.
But this afternoon by the lion's cage
I'm afraid I got too near.
And I'm writing these lines
From inside a lion,
And it's rather dark in here.

Shel Silverstein

THINK OF EIGHT NUMBERS

Think of eight numbers from one to nine –
That's fine.
Now pick up the phone and dial them all –
That's making a call.
Now wait till somebody answers,
Then shout 'Yickety-yick!' and hang up
   quick,
And sit for awhile,
And have a smile,
And start all over again.

Shel Silverstein

BRIAN

Brian is a baddie,
As nasty as they come.
He terrifies his daddy
And mortifies his mum.

One morning in December
They took him to the zoo,

But Brian lost his temper
And kicked a kangaroo.

And then he fought a lion
Escaping from its pit.
It tried to swallow Brian
Till Brian swallowed it!

Yes, Brian is a devil,
A horrid little curse –
Unlike his brother Neville
Who's infinitely worse!

Doug Macleod

THE BALLAD OF DARREN CULLEN

This is the case of Darren Cullen
    (Blue eyes, six foot three),
His Dad, his teacher (Mrs Spence)
    And his headmaster (me).

Big Darren's Daddy picked him up
    When the lad was two foot tall
And swung him by the ankles hard
    Against the bedroom wall.

Young Darren leaned around the back
    Of the Star and Garter Inn
While his Daddy bought his Auntie Chris
    Her seventh double gin.

And when the boy was five foot tall
    They caught him in Grigson's Yard
Driving a forklift truck around
    The piles of packing card.

Down by the gloomiest canal
    In the gloomiest weather
Darren reached the start of his youth
    And the end of his short tether.

His teacher, knowing the school was built
    For her own peace and quiet,
Gently tickled in him one day
    His tendency to riot.

'Nobody loves you Darren Cullen
  And I will tell you why . . . '
She said, and found no going on
  For the death in Darren's eye.

He's taken from a new display
  Of farming implements
A horse mane docker, and it's aimed
  At Mrs Muriel Spence.

The headmaster's praying suddenly
  And his lunge is rather tardy –
The thing is sticking neatly out
  Of Mrs Spence's cardy.

After a vivid afternoon
  They found out what you've guessed –
The horse mane docker hardly got
  Beyond Mu Spence's vest.

Thank God, we said. Darren was carted
  Off to special school
For scaring a teacher witless with
  An agricultural tool.

These days the lad is six foot three
  And he takes his revenge on all
His women nightly, and the little boy
  That he bangs on the bedroom wall.

                              Fred Sedgwick

LIZZIE AND THE APPLE TREE

Once upon a time,
Every day for a while,
Lizzie sat up in the apple tree
Behind the leaves
And a smile,

And she said when they called
That she wouldn't come down
Till the apples dropped off
And the leaves turned brown.

She swung her legs
And laughed at their frown
And didn't come down
Didn't come down.

Lizzie sat up in
The apple tree's hair
In the wind and the rain
In the sun and the air.

Lizzie swung in
the apple tree's arms
And ignored her family's
Tempers and charms,

When Lizzie turned into an apple
They ceased to scold and berate her
And when the apples fell down
They forgot she was Lizzie –
And ate her!

Julie Holder

HOME HAIRCUT

Nellie, cutting Johnnie's hair,
Was taking insufficient care;
She turned to hear what someone said,
And found that she'd cut off his head!
She smiled, 'I know just what to do,'
And stuck it on again with glue.

John Cunliffe

Hayley is a nice person.
At playtime she is my friend
and during lessons I help her.
She is no good at sums
and can't spell proper.
She has little blue eyes
and she eats too much.
When she yells she goes all red,
her face swells up,
her eyes pop,
and she tells **LIES** –
like wen she came bak from
play jus now
and sed Im not yore frend no more
yuv a bad temper
i saw what you writ
Well im not yore frend neather
your NASTY Haily!!!

A good start, Justine,
but for some reason
your spelling went off towards the end.

Brian Morse

Little Suzy Armitage
was brilliant from an early age.
In every way in all endeavour,
she was particularly clever.
Before she reached the age of two
(when normal babies only 'goo')
she learned to count, and read and write
much to her parents' delight.
She mastered algebra at three
and learned about geometry
at four. Her father, very glad,
said, 'Yes, she gets it from her dad!'
Her mother had to disagree:
'Our daughter gets her brains from me!'

At twelve it had become the rule
that people came to Suzy's school
in numbers that were epidemic.
Suzy, smiling sweetly bright,
gave answers that were always right!

In case you think that Suzy's skill
was lots of fun . . . it made her ill!
Instead those big blue eyes so clear,
were troubled by a secret fear:
Deep down, she knew, before too long,
that she must get an answer wrong!
So Suzy knew she had to make
a quite deliberate mistake.
(For everybody makes one once,
from genius to dullest dunce.)

So all day long she bent her mind
to matters of a phoney kind,
and finally, young Suzy said
(And proudly, too!) 'The sky is red!'

Knowing her mistake was past
she, happy and relaxed, fell fast
asleep – but in the black of night
a straying iron meteorite
got all burnt up to ashy dust
and stained the stratosphere with rust.
So when poor Suzy left her bed
next day – Alas! The sky was red!
And people said: 'The truth is out –
that girl is *always right*, no doubt!'

So Suzy tried to make abatement
by spouting quite the daftest statement.
She said: 'Our garden birds can't fly!'
(She hadn't noticed passing by,
A van with penguins from the zoo
had broken down, with doors askew,
and dozens of the flightless creatures
were eating grandmother's prize freesias.)
So poor old Suzy's plan had failed;
What could she do? she wailed and wailed.
She summoned every ounce courageous,
saying something quite outrageous.
'I', she thought, 'will tell them that
I think it's true the world is flat!'

It was across the headlines plastered,
and everyone was flabbergasted.

But Suzy was so much relieved,
that rubbish couldn't be believed!
She needn't worry any longer
about the threat of being wrong.
A feeling like a royal pardon
sent her, free, into the garden.
But, just beyond the privet hedge,
she discovered the end of the world
and fell off the
                 e
                  d
                   g
                    e
                     !

Joanne Fowdy

CLIVE COTTER

The new boy –
Clive Cotter –
broke my pencil,
hid my rubber.

Moved my chair
and made me fall,
wrote my name
on the toilet wall.

Terror of the playground,
worst that you'll meet –
Clive Cotter,
the dirty rotter.

Called me a liar,
made me a fool,
took my crisps,
broke every rule.

But now he's my friend!
My best friend!
How did it happen?
A fight

in the playground
neither could win,
both kept in –
be friends you two!

I fought him,
Clive fought me,
his mother invited me
home to tea!

Terrors of the street,
worst that you'll meet –
two dirty rotters,
two Clive Cotters!

Brian Morse

MUMS AND DADS

NUC has just passed a weighty resolution:
'Unless all parents raise our rate of pay
This action will be taken by our members
(The resolution comes in force today): –

'Noses will not be blown (sniffs are in
    order),
Bedtime will get preposterously late,
Ice-cream and crisps will be consumed for
    breakfast,
Unwanted cabbage left upon the plate,

'Earholes and fingernails can't be inspected,
Overtime (known as homework) won't be
    worked,
Reports from school will all say "Could do
    better",
Putting bricks back in boxes may be
    shirked.'

THE NATIONAL ASSOCIATION OF PARENTS

Of course, NAP's answer quickly was
    forthcoming
(It was a matter of emergency),
It issued to the Press the following
    statement
(Its Secretary appeared on TV): –

'True that the so-called Saturday allowance
Hasn't kept pace with prices in the shops,
But neither have, alas, parental wages:
NUC's claim would ruin kind, hard-
    working Pops.

'Therefore, unless that claim is now
    abandoned,
Strike action for us, too, is what remains;
In planning for the which we are in process
Of issuing, to all our members, canes.'

Roy Fuller

THE PARENT

Children aren't happy with nothing to
    ignore,
And that's what parents were created for.

Ogden Nash

HOW TO SCARE YOUR PARENTS

Bang your head upon your knee
Hang yourself upon a tree
Pull your legs out of their sockets
Now put fire works in your pockets
Go upstairs and go to bed
And make believe that you are dead.

Thomas Joseph Divine (8)

ALL FOR AN ICE-CREAM

'Mum, can I have an ice-cream?'
'Go ask your dad.'
'Dad, can I have an ice-cream?'

'Go ask your mum.'
'But I've just asked her and she told me to
    ask you.'
'Well tell her that I've told you to ask her.'
'Mum, dad's just told me to tell you that
    you've
got to tell me if I can have an ice.'
'Oh well I suppose you can but go ask your
    dad
for 10p.'
'Right.'
'Dad, can I have 10p for an ice-cream?'
'I haven't got 10p.'
'Oh come on dad you haven't looked yet
    and oh
hurry the van'll go soon.'
'Let's have a look then, ah, there you are.'
'Thanks dad, Ohh!'
'What's matter now!'
'The van's gone.'

Karen Jackson

My parents grew among palmtrees,
in sunshine strong and clear.
I grow in weather that's pale,
misty, watery or plain cold,
around back streets of London.

Dad swam in warm sea, at my age.
I swim in a roofed pool.
Mum – she still doesn't swim.

Mum went to an open village market
at my age. I go to a covered
arcade one with her now.
Dad works most Saturdays.

At my age Dad played
cricket with friends.
Mum helped her mum, or talked
shouting halfway up a hill.
Now I read or talk on the phone.

With her friends Mum's mum washed
clothes on a river-stone. Now
washing-machine washes our clothes.
We save time to eat to TV,
never speaking.

My dad longed for a freedom in Jamaica.
I want a greater freedom.
Mum prays for us, always.

Mum goes to church
some evenings and Sundays.
I go to the library.
Dad goes for his darts at the local.

Mum walked everywhere, at my age.
Dad rode a donkey.
Now I take a bus
or catch the underground train.

James Berry

MOTHER'S NERVES

My mother said, 'If just once more
I hear you slam that old screen door,
I'll tear out my hair! I'll dive in the stove!'
I gave it a bang and in she dove.

X. J. Kennedy

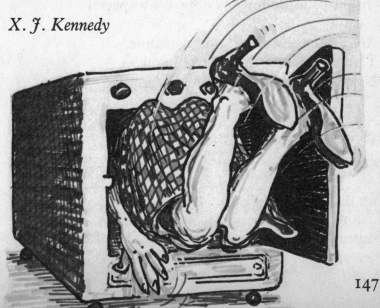

Why did you do it, Mother?
I told you – didn't I – that I'd go with you
to a restaurant for my birthday
on one condition: Don't go and blab
to the waitress it's my **BIG DAY**.
But you had to go and tell her.
God, what if somebody had seen me?
I realise that you and Daddy
simply do not care if you ruin my
   reputation.
I almost thought for a teensy second
you had restrained yourself for once.
But no. You and your big mouth.
'Hip, hop, happy, b, birth, day,
hap, hap, happy, Happy Birthday to You!':
a zero girl, singing a zero song
at the top of her nothingness of a voice.
'All of us at Bennigans hope it's a special
   day!'
All of them, Mother, not just some.
That's IT for birthdays from now on.
Next year I'll be celebrating by myself.

                    Julia O'Callaghan

I LOVE ME MUDDER . . .

I love me mudder and me mudder love me
we come so far from over de sea,
we heard dat de streets were paved with
   gold
sometime it hot sometime it cold
I love me mudder and me mudder love me
we try fe live in harmony
you might know her as Valerie
but to me she is my mummy.

She shouts at me daddy so loud some time
she don't smoke weed she don't drink wine
she always do the best she can
she work damn hard down ina England,
she's always singing some kind of song
she have big muscles and she very very
   strong
she likes pussy cats and she love cashew
   nuts
she don't bother with no if and buts.

I love me mudder and me mudder love me
we come so far from over de sea
we heard dat de streets were paved with
   gold
sometime it hot sometime it cold,
I love her and she love me too
and dis is a love I know is true
me and my mudder we love you too.

Benjamin Zephaniah

THE GERBIL

'Can we have a gerbil, mum?'
'We can't,' is what mum said.
'I'm sorry, love,' she added,
'I'm having a baby, instead.'

'I'd rather have a
    gerbil, mum,
I'd like a pet,' I said.
But what I'll get is a
    baby,
With a face all
    screaming and red.

'I'll tell you what,'
    said mother,
'I'll tell you what
    we'll do.
If you help me with
    the baby,
You can have a gerbil, too.'

I got the gerbil I wanted,
And I help mum every day.
The baby isn't too bad –
But the gerbil's quieter, I'd say.

Tony Bradman

GIVE UP SLIMMING, MUM

My mum
is short
and plump
and pretty
and I wish
she'd give up
slimming.

So does Dad.

Her cooking's
delicious –
you can't
beat it –
but you really can –
hardly bear
to eat it –
the way she sits
with her eyes
brimming,

watching you
polish off
the spuds
and trimmings
while she
has nothing
herself but a small
thin dry
diet biscuit:
that's all.

My mum
is short
and plump
and pretty
and I wish
she'd give up
slimming.

So does Dad.

She says she
looks as though
someone had
sat on her –
BUT WE LIKE MUM
WITH A BIT
OF FAT ON HER!

Kit Wright

TARDINESS

Goodness gracious sakes alive!
Mother said, 'Come home at five!'
Now the clock is striking six,
I am in a norful fix!
She will think I can't be trusted,
And she'll say that she's disgusted!

Gelett Burgess

GROTTY BORLOTTI

Mum went to a lecture and gave up meat.
Now she dishes up beans, 'just for a treat',
we get –

Creamy bran chunks or buckwheat bake,
brandied prune mousse and carrot cake.

Hazelnut tart with stir fried cheese,
garlic salad and herbal teas.

Mushroom paté and split pea spread,
soya burger on curried bread.

Wholemeal pasta and a broadbean nutlet,
cashew nut soup and a chick pea cutlet.

Continental lentil or rice on toast,
grotty borlotti and dreaded nut roast.

Coconut chutney and beanshoot fritters.
It's boring beans that give us the jitters.

So, Dad and I took up jogging,
just down to the end of the street.
For it isn't too far
to the Hamburger Bar,
where, 'just for a treat',
we'll stop –
and eat meat.

Pie Corbett

ONE PARENT FAMILY

My mum says she's clueless
not, as you'd imagine,
at wiring three pin plugs or
straightening a bicycle wheel,
but at sewing buttons
on a shirt, icing names and
dates on birthday cakes,
preparing a three course meal.

She's not like other mothers;
although she's slim and neat
she looks silly in an apron,
just great in dungarees.
She'll tackle any household job,
lay lino, fix on tiles, does
all the outside paintwork, climbs
a ladder with practised ease.

Mind you, she's good for
a cuddle when I fall and
cut my knee. She tells me
fantastic stories every night,
laughs at *my* disasters, says
that she's as bad when she
reads a recipe all wrong and
her cakes don't come out right.

I know on open evenings
she gives a bad impression
at the school. She doesn't wear
the proper clothes. 'Too bad,'

the others sometimes say,
'You've got such a peculiar mum.'
'It's just as well,' I tell them.
'She is my mother *and* my dad!'

Moira Andrew

WHY?

Why are the leaves always green, Dad?
Why are there thorns on a rose?
Why do you want my neck clean, Dad?
Why do hairs grow from your nose?

Why can dogs hear what we can't, Dad?
Why has the engine just stalled?
Why are you rude about Aunt, Dad?
Why are you going all bald?

Why is Mum taller than you, Dad?
Why can't the dog stand the cat?
Why's Grandma got a moustache, Dad?
Why are you growing more fat?

Why don't you answer my questions?
You used to; you don't any more.
Why? Tell me why, Tell me why, Dad?
Do you think I am being a bore?

John Kitching

HOT FOOD

We sit down to eat
and the potato's a bit hot
so I only put a little bit on my fork
and I blow
whooph whooph
until it's cool
just cool
then into the mouth
nice.
And there's my brother
he's doing the same
whooph whooph
into the mouth
nice.
There's my mum
she's doing the same
whooph whooph
into the mouth
nice.

But my dad.
My dad.
What does he do?
He stuffs a great big chunk of potato
into his mouth,
then
that really does it.
His eyes pop out
he flaps his hands
he blows, he puffs, he yells
he bobs his head up and down

he spits bits of potato
all over his plate
and he turns to us and he says,
'Watch out everybody –
the potato's very hot.'

Michael Rosen

BUTTERFINGERS

When father finished up his toast
he raised his plate for more
so mother buttered some and said,
'Don't drop it on the floor.'
'I'm not a little child!' he cried.
'I never drop my toast,'
then tipped it over on the mat . . .
    and mother laughed the most.

Peggy Dunstan

D.I.Y. MAN

Dad's a hobbyist, a hobby man.
Every moment he can
is spent on his latest fad,
ruling his life, driving us mad.

He's been into computers, and cars,
and home-made wine in enormous jars.
His latest is tropical freshwater fish –
they're the answer to his fairy godmother's
    wish.

The garden's a desert, a waste,
since herbaceous borders became his taste.
Nine times out of ten we have to catch the
    bus –
he blames losing the car manual on us.

The sight of a new magazine is a sad
and certain sign that yet again he's got it
    bad.
'Your family's an abandoned hobby,' Mum
    sighs.
'Let's face it we could have turned into flies

on the wall of that shed you bought
for the fancy pigeons which caught
your eye at that show. And as for the hi-fi
    it's the same –
Hey! Are you listening? Do you remember
    my name?'

'Pardon?' Dad says, ever so politely,
raising his head. 'A new idea's just struck
    me.'

                              Brian Morse

PARENTS' SAYINGS

My mum sometimes says:
'Shut your mouth and eat your dinner!'
Which I think is pretty impossible.
And sometimes she says:
'Do you know what a knife and fork are?'
Or, 'You drink that pop as if it's going out
    of fashion!'

If I climb a ladder to try and get my ball
    down
from the gutter, or if I'm sitting on a wall,
She shouts:
'If you fall off that and break both your legs
    don't come running to me!'
(As if I could do that.)

When it rains and I get ready to go out,
My dad says:
'You're not going out until you've done
    your homework!'
And I say: 'I've done it'. He says:
'You're still not going out!'
I just don't understand my parents
    sometimes.
                        Zoe Horsley (13)

CLAIMS

My father had a motor car:
It was his pride and joy.
He would have taught me how to drive
If I had been a boy.

But girls grow into women
And women are to blame,
According to my father,
For each insurance claim.

We're just not built for things like cars.
Dad says we mustn't moan:
Men are built for speed and strength,
Women for the home.

My mother used to drive a bit
Until the accident:
Parking in the multi-storey,
A wing mirror got bent.

It wasn't really Mum's fault,
There simply wasn't space.
You'd think to hear my father rant
She'd damned the human race.

My mother didn't argue,
She says she saves her breath,
Dad homes in for a blazing row
Like vultures swoop on death.

'Women drivers,' said my dad
'No one need discuss:
Women should accept their lot
And meekly take the bus.'

Which makes it such a pity,
Such wretched awful luck,
That Dad has driven his new car
Halfway up a truck.

What makes it worse in Dad's eyes
(And the police's book)
Is that the truck was neatly parked
And father didn't look.

His seat belt meant that he was safe,
Though the car's beyond repair;
What hurt him was the firemen laughed
As they cut him free from there.

He sometimes takes the subject up,
Explains the crash away.
My Mum and I say nothing,
Much to Dad's dismay.

But part of what Dad taught me,
I must admit, remains:
Men are built for speed and strength
But hardly any brains.

David Kitchen

IRRITATING SAYINGS

Isn't it time you thought about bed?
    It must be somewhere
You speak to him Harold, he won't
        listen to me.
    Who do you think I am?
You'd better ask your father
    It's late enough as it is
Don't eat with your mouth open
    In this day and age
Did anybody ask your opinion
    I remember when I was a boy
        And after all we do for you

You're not talking to your school friends
  now you know
       Why don't you do it the proper
       way
      I'm only trying to tell you
       What did I just say
     Now, wrap up warm
      B.E.D. spells bed
    Sit up straight and don't gobble your
    food
       For the five hundredth time
Don't let me ever see you do that again.
     Have you made your bed?
Can't you look further than your nose?
       No more lip
Have you done your homework?

    Because I say so.
   Don't come those fancy ways here
  Any more and you'll be in bed
My, haven't you grown
Some day I won't be here, then you'll see
    A chair's for sitting on
  You shouldn't need telling at your age.
Want, want, want, that's all you ever say.

collated by David Jackson

163

Most parents like their holidays to be a cosy
    rest,
They think a nice relaxing place, with
    sunshine, is best.
But my Dad is quite different, he's very
    energetic
And holidays we spend with him, are bound
    to be athletic.

We've clambered up Ben Nevis, and we've
    tramped across the moors,
When many times we've wished, we could
    have stayed behind, indoors.
Last year we made a protest; said we'd
    stretch out in the sun,
And Dad must like it or lump it – that was
    our idea of fun!

I think he was surprised, because he just
    stood there and mumbled.
As we reached the Grand Hotel, he never
    even grumbled.
He sat down on the beach with us, and
    gazed right out to sea,
Spread suntan oil upon our backs as calmly
    as can be.

At first we were delighted, as we lay there in
    the sand.
With everything, we thought, conveniently
    at hand.

But after three whole days, that small
   suspicion gnawed
And finally, we realised the truth – that we
   were bored!

Mum began to fidget, she put aside her
   knitting,
My sister sighed and scowled a lot, I knew
   their teeth were gritting.
We didn't dare complain, for what we
   wanted most, we had,
Yet, happy as a sandboy in the sunshine lay
   our Dad!

Then my Dad began to smile – the smile
   became a grin,
'Why don't you all admit you're bored,' he
   said, 'it's not a sin!
I went out for a walk last night, and found a
   riding stable,
We'll spend the next week trekking, if you
   all feel fit and able!'

Now we've learnt that holidays without
   much kind of action
Cannot give us what we need, in terms of
   satisfaction.
Dad's ideas may cause us all to grumble or
   to joke,
But deckchairs on the beach can stay there,
   for other folk!

Christine Ann Farrell

DAD'S PIGEON

Now pigeon-racing is a sport
That dad was keen on trying.
Alas, the bird that daddy bought
Was terrified of flying.

'Well, who's a pretty pigeon then?'
Said daddy, as he threw it.
The pigeon fell to earth again;
'You twit!' cried dad. 'You blew it!'

'You've got to flap your wings,' said dad.
'Now practise, get acquainted!'
The pigeon flapped its wings
    like mad,
Took off, then promptly fainted.

To help the pigeon understand
Dad gave a demonstration,
He flapped, he jumped and came
    to land
In mother's rose plantation.

My dad is slowly on the mend,
My mother's still in shock,
And me? I take our feathered
    friend
For walkies round the block.

Doug
Macleod

FATHER SAYS

Father says
Never
let
me
see
you
doing
that
again
father says
tell you once
tell you a thousand times
come hell or high water
his finger drills my shoulder
never let me see you doing that again

My brother knows all his phrases off by
    heart
so we practise them in bed at night.

Michael Rosen

TA-RA MAM

Ta-ra mam.
Can you hear me? I'm going out to play.
I've got me playing-out clothes on
and me wellies.
What d'yer say?
Oh! I'm going to the cow-field.

I'm going with me mates.
Yes! I know tea's nearly ready.
I promise I won't be late.

Anyway, what we havin'?
Can't I have beans on toast?
What d'yer mean, mam, summat proper?
I ate me dinner (almost).
No, I won't go anywhere lonely,
and I'm going with Chris and Jackie,
so if anyone gets funny
we can all do our karate!

Yer what?
(Oh blimey. Here we go again.)
No, I won't go near the river.
I know we've had too much rain
and I won't go in the newsagent's
trying to nick the sweets.
Yer what, mam? I'm not. Honest.
I'm not trying to give yer cheek.

Wait mam.
Hang on a minute. Chris is here in the hall.
He says summat good's on the telly,
so I think I'll stay in after all!

Brenda Leather

We don't have ghosts in our house. That
   noise
is just Mum creeping downstairs for crisps
   in the dark.

In the hall she puts the light on to avoid the
   Hoover
so you know it's her and not – well, you
   know.

Then you hear Dad waking and groaning,
'What on earth!' and out of bed he gets too.

And here's Mum at the bottom of the stairs
with her rustling bag of crisps whispering
   ever so loud:

'Why are you up? I didn't mean to wake
   you,'
and Dad says, resigned, 'The bed was cold.

And what's the use of dieting in the day
if you eat all night?' 'I was hungry,' Mum
   says.

(You'd think by now she'd got a better
   answer than that
but she hasn't.) 'The whole point about
   dieting is,'

Dad says, 'but I won't expand.'
'I'll go without my breakfast,' Mum says,
    'honestly.'

'I bet,' Dad says and goes downstairs too.
By now my elder sister Tracey has woken

and is stumbling to the toilet. She slams the
    door
and slams it on the way back and slams her
    own door.

'Listen! You've woken Tracey up,' Dad
    says very clearly.
'You know what she's like in the morning

if she doesn't get her beauty sleep.
    Venomous!
The next thing – oh speak of the devil!'
    That's me.

'Haven't I ever told you – ONCE IN BED
    STAY THERE?
Do you know what time it is?' 'You woke
    me,' I say

in my sleepy little kid's voice that
    sometimes fools him.
Luckily the canaries choose that moment to
    start chirping

their morning chorus. The kettle boils. 'Tea
    or coffee?'

Dad asks. 'I think I might have beans,'
  Mum says

like something exotic. By now I'm loading
  up the toaster.
'I've got to be up in six hours,' Dad
  grumbles.

'Two sugared, one with saccharin. I'll have
  three slices
with butter – none of that slimming
  margarine nonsense.'

'Me too,' Mum says. 'I'll go back on my
  diet tomorrow.'
'The day after tomorrow,' Dad yawns. 'The
  day after.'

Brian Morse

MY OBNOXIOUS BROTHER

My obnoxious brother Bobby
Has a most revolting hobby;
There, behind the garden wall is
Where he captures creepy-crawlies.

Grannies, aunts and baby cousins
Come to our house in their dozens,
But they disappear discreetly
When they see him smiling sweetly.

For they know, as he approaches,
In his pockets are cockroaches,
Spiders, centipedes and suchlike;
All of which they do not much like.

As they head towards the lobby,
Bidding fond farewells to Bobby,
How they wish he'd change his habits
And keep guinea pigs or rabbits.

But their wishes are quite futile,
For he thinks that bugs are cute. I'll
Finish now, but just remind you:
Bobby could be right
behind you!

Colin West

WASHING UP

On Sundays,
my mum and dad said,
'Right, we've cooked the dinner,
you two can wash it up,'
and then they went off to the front room.

So then we began.
First there was the row about who
was to wash and who was to dry.
My brother said, 'You're too slow at
    washing,
I have to hang about waiting for you,'
so I said,
'You always wash, it's not fair.'

'Hard cheese,' he says.
'I'm doing it.'
So that was that.

'Whoever dries has to stack the dishes,'
he says,
so that's me stacking the dishes
while he's getting the water ready.

Now,
quite often we used to have mustard
with our Sunday dinner
and we didn't have it out of a tube,
one of us used to make it with the powder
in an eggcup

and there was nearly always
some left over.

Anyway,
my brother
he'd be washing up by now
and he's standing there at the sink
his hands in the water,
I'm drying up,
and suddenly he goes,
'Quick, quick quick
come over here
quick, you'll miss it
quick, you'll miss it.'
'What?' I say, 'What?'
'Quick, quick. In here,
in the water.'
I say,

'What? What?'
'Give us your hand,' he says
and he grabs my hand
then my finger,
'What?' I say,
'That,' he says,
and he pulls my finger under the water
and stuffs it into the eggcup
with left-over blobs of old mustard
stuck to the bottom.
It's all slimy.
'Oh Horrible.'

I was an idiot to have believed him.
So I go on drying up.

Suddenly
I feel a little speck of water on my neck.
I look up at the ceiling.
Where'd that come from?

I look at my brother
he's grinning all over his big face.

'Oy, cut that out,'
He grins again
sticks his finger under the water
in the bowl and
flicks.

Plip.
'Oy, that got me right on my face.'
'Did it? did it? did it?'
He's well pleased.

So now it's my turn
I've got the drying up cloth, haven't I?
And I've been practising for ages
on the kitchen door handle.
Now he's got his back to me
washing up
and
out goes the cloth, like a whip, it goes
right on the –
'Ow – that hurt. I didn't hurt *you*.'
Now it's me grinning.

So he goes,
'All right, let's call it quits.'
'OK,' I say, 'one-all. Fairy squarey.'

So I go on drying up.
What I don't know is that
he's got the Fairy Liquid bottle under the
water
boop boop boop boop boop boop
it's filling up
with dirty soapy water
and next thing it's out of the water
and he's gone squeeesh
and squirted it right in my face.

'Got you in the mush,' he goes.

'Right, that's it,' I say,
'I've had enough.'
And I go upstairs and get
this old bicycle cape I've got,
one of those capes you can wear
when you ride a bicycle in the rain.

So I come down in that
and I say,
'OK I'm ready for anything you've got now.
You can't get me now, can you?'

So next thing he's got the little
washing-up brush
and it's got little bits of meat fat
and squashed peas stuck in it
and he's come up to me
and he's in, up, under the cape with it
working it round and round
under my jumper, and under my chin.

So that makes me really wild
and I make a grab for anything that'll
hold water; dip it in the sink
and fling it at him.

What I don't know is that
while I went upstairs to get the cape
he's got a secret weapon ready.

It's his bicycle pump,
he's loaded it with the dirty washing-up
   water
by sucking it all in.
He picks it up,
and it's squirt again.
All over my hair.

Suddenly the door opens.
'Have you finished the . . . ?'
It's Mum **AND** Dad.

'Just look at this.
Look at the pair of them.'

And there's water all over the floor
all over the table
and all we've washed up is
two plates and the mustard pot.

My dad says,
'You can't be trusted to do anything you're
   asked,
can you?'

He always says that.

Mind you, the floor was pretty clean
after we had mopped it all up.

Michael Rosen

MY SISTER BETTY

My sister Betty said,
'I'm going to be a famous actress.'
Last year she was going to be a missionary.
'Famous actresses always look unhappy but
    beautiful,'
She said pulling her mouth sideways
And making her eyes turn upwards
So they were mostly white.
'Do I look unhappy but beautiful?'
'I want to go to bed and read,' I said.
'Famous actresses suffer and have
    hysterics,' she said.
'I've been practising my hysterics.'
She began going very red and screaming
So that it hurt my ears.
She hit herself on the head with her fists
And rolled off my bed onto the lino.
I stood by the wardrobe where it was safer.
She got up saying, 'Thank you, thank you.'
And bowed to the four corners of my
    bedroom.
'Would you like an encore of hysterics?' she
    asked.

'No,' I said from inside the wardrobe.
There was fluff all over her vest.
'If you don't clap enthusiastically,' she said,
'I'll put your light out when you're reading.'
While I clapped a bit
She bowed and shouted, 'More, more.'
My mother shouted upstairs,
'Go to bed and stop teasing, Betty.'
'The best thing about being a famous
    actress,' Betty said,
'Is that you die a lot.'
She fell to the floor with a crash
And lay there for an hour and a half
With her eyes staring at the ceiling.
She only went away when I said,
'You really look like a famous actress.'

When I got into bed and started reading
She came and switched off my light.
It's not much fun
Having a famous actress for a sister.

Gareth Owen

WILLIE BUILT A GUILLOTINE

Willie built a guillotine,
Tried it out on sister Jean.
Said Mother as she got the mop:
'These messy games have got to stop!'

William E. Engel

SAMMY

I wish I was our Sammy
Our Sammy's nearly ten.
He's got two worms and a catapult
An' he's built a underground den.
But I'm not allowed to go in there,
I have to stay near the gate,
'Cos me Mam says I'm only seven,
But I'm not, I'm nearly eight!

I sometimes hate our Sammy,
He robbed me toy car y'know,
Now the wheels are missin' an' the top's
    broke off,
An' the bleedin' thing won' go.
An' he said when he took it, it was just like
    that,
But it wasn't, it went dead straight,
But y' can't say nott'n when they think y'
    seven
An' y' not, y' nearly eight.

I wish I was our Sammy,
Y' wanna see him spit,
Straight in y' eye from twenty yards
An' every time a hit.
He's allowed to play with matches,
And he goes to bed dead late,
And I have to go at seven,
Even though I'm nearly eight.

Y' know our Sammy,
He draws nudey women,
Without arms, or legs, or even heads
In the baths, when he goes swimmin'.
But I'm not allowed to go to the baths,
Me Mam says I have to wait,
'Cos I might get drowned, 'cos I'm only
   seven,
But I'm not, I'm nearly eight.

Y' know our Sammy,
Y' know what he sometimes does?
He wees straight through the letter box
Of the house next door to us.
I tried to do it one night,
But I had to stand on a crate,
'Cos I couldn't reach
   the letter box
But I will by the
   time I'm eight.

Willie Russell

RELATIVELY SPEAKING

SWAP? SELL? SMALL ADS SELL FAST!

1956 Dad. Good runner; needs one or
Two repairs; a few grey hairs but
Nothing a respray couldn't fix
Would like a 1966 five speed turbo
In exchange: something in the sporty
Twin-carb range.

1920s Granny. Not many like this
In such clean and rust free state.
You must stop by to view! All chrome
As new, original fascia retained
Upholstery unstained. Passed **MOT**
Last week: will only swap for some-
Thing quite unique.

1993 low mileage Brother. As eco-
Nomical as any other. Must mention
Does need some attention. Stream-
Lined, rear spoiler. Runs on milk
Baby oil and gripe water. Serviced;
Needs rear wash/wipe. Only one
Owner; not yet run in. Will swap
For anything.

Trevor Millum

ORDERS OF THE DAY

Get up!
Get washed!
Eat your breakfast!
That's my mum,
Going on and on and on and on . . .

Sit down!
Shut up!
Get on with your work!
That's my teacher,
Going on and on and on and on . . .

Come here!
Give me that!
Go away!
That's my big sister,
Going on and on and on and on . . .

Get off!
Stop it!
Carry me!
That's my little sister,
Going on and on and on and on . . .

Boss
Boss
Boss
They do it all day.
Sometimes I think I'll run away,
But I don't know

Where to go.

The only one who doesn't do it,
Is my old gran.
She says,
'Would you like to get washed?'
Or,
'Would you like to sit on this chair?'
And she listens to what I say.
People say she spoils me,
And that she's old-fashioned.
I think it's the others that spoil;
They spoil every day.
And I wish more people were old-fashioned,
. . . like my gran.

John Cunliffe

NEVER A DULL MOMENT

If you like to keep lively,
If you hate being bored,
Just come down to our house
And knock on the door.

It's the noisiest house
In the whole of our town,
There's doors always slamming
And things falling down.

There's my dad, who keeps shouting,
And my mum, who breaks things,
The baby (who'll bite you!)
And our dog running rings.

There's my sister the screamer
And my brother who roars,
And a grandpa who's stone deaf
(He's the one who slams doors).

So come down to our house,
You don't need the address,
You'll hear it ten miles away
And the outside's a mess.

You won't mind the racket,
You'll just love the din –
For there's never a dull moment
In the house *we* live in!

Tony Bradman

I ring the bell,
Then ring it again,
Into the hall comes Auntie Jane,
She flings the door open wide,
She asks us all to come inside.
I hold my breath and count to three,
I know what lies ahead of me,
Uncle Bill is in his chair,
Cousin Bob is over there.
And Dolores and Rich from the US of A
They are also on their way.
Nieces and nephews,
Relatives galore,
Start to pile in through the door.
'Oh, look at her size,'
'Hasn't she grown!'
Uncle Albert is on the phone.
They all start to gossip,
Through photos they flick,
All of a sudden I want to be sick.
Through all the photographs they thumb,
Auntie Mo's got a boil on her bum,
Uncle Cyril's got constipation,
And Auntie Jean's had her operation.
'Tea is ready,' I hear Auntie Jane shout,
And one by one we all file out,
We all eat our tea while Dolores brags,
Cyril complains and Auntie Jean nags.
All I can do is sit and eat,
Rodney complains about his feet,
Little Barney strangles the cat,

And hits the dog with a cricket bat.
Uncle Albert slurps his tea,
And little Margaret wants a wee.
In comes the jelly, I watch it quiver,
John's heart is bad and so is his liver.
Everyone takes their share of the jelly,
Barney spoons ice-cream into the telly,
Sidney eats pickles out of the jar,
Uncle Tom smokes his cigar.
Barney plays with Uncle Bill's bowls,
He gets his fingers stuck in the holes,
Everyone tries to get Barney unstuck,
I'm bored so I read the telephone book.
Auntie Dolores brags away,
'We got some more servants the other day,'
Uncle Bob drinks his beer,
Martha is pregnant again we hear.
Albert does his party piece,
He's a magician he saws up my niece.
The bathroom isn't vacant yet,
It's been quite full since the Crepes Suzette.
The night is coming to an end,
I think I'm going round the bend,
Goodnights are said with hugs and tears,
I'm glad I won't see this lot for another few
    years.

Joanne Potter (14)

CHILDREN WITH ADULTS

My auntie gives me a colouring book and
    crayons.
I begin to colour.
After a while she looks over to see what I
    have done and says
you've gone over the lines
that's what you've done.
What do you think they're there for, ay?
Some kind of statement is it?
Going to be a rebel are we?
I begin to cry.
My uncle gives me a hanky and some blank
    paper
do your own designs he says
I begin to colour.
When I have done he looks over and tells
    me they are all very
good.
He is lying,
only some of them are.

John Hegley

STARTER

Hi!
I'm cousin Art,
And I like to start
A new thing every day.
But I never finish anything;
At least that's what . . . they . . .

Tony Bradman

My Uncle Dan's an inventor, you may think
    that's very fine.
You may wish he was your Uncle instead of
    being mine –
If he wanted he could make a watch that
    bounces when it drops,
He could make a helicopter out of string
    and bottle tops
Or any really useful thing you can't get in
    the shops.
But Uncle Dan has other ideas:
The bottomless glass for ginger beers,
The toothless saw that's safe for the tree,
A special word for a spelling bee
(Like Lionocerangoutangadder),
Or the roll-uppable rubber ladder,
The mystery pie that bites when it's bit –
My Uncle Dan invented it.
My Uncle Dan sits in his den inventing
    night and day.
His eyes peer from his hair and beard like
    mice from a load of hay.
And does he make the shoes that will go
    walks without your feet?
A shrinker to shrink instantly the elephants
    you meet?
A carver that just carves from the air steaks
    cooked and ready to eat?
No, no, he has other intentions –
Only perfectly useless inventions:
Glassless windows (they never break),

A medicine to cure the earthquake,
The unspillable screwed-down cup,
The stairs that go neither down nor up,
The door you simply paint on a wall –
Uncle Dan invented them all.

Ted Hughes

UNCLE ED'S HEADS

Fame was a claim of Uncle Ed's,
Simply because he had three heads,
Which, if he'd only had a third of,
I think he would never have been heard of.

Ogden Nash

UNCLE ALBERT

When I was almost eight years old
My Uncle Albert came to stay;
He wore a watch-chain made of gold
And sometimes he would let me play
With both the chain and gleaming watch,
And though at times I might be rough
He never seemed to bother much.
He smelled of shaving-soap and snuff.
To me he was a kind of God,
Immensely wise and strong and kind,
And so I thought it rather odd
When I came home from school to find
Two strangers, menacing and tall,
In the parlour, looking grim
As Albert – suddenly quite small –
Let them rudely hustle him
Out to where a black car stood.
Both Albert and his
   watch and chain
Disappeared that
   day for good.
My parents said
   he'd gone to
   Spain.

Vernon Scannell

CHRISTMAS THANK YOUS

Dear Auntie
Oh, what a nice jumper
I've always adored powder blue
and fancy you thinking of
orange and pink
for the stripes
how clever of you

Dear Uncle
The soap is
terrific
So
useful
and such a kind thought and
how did you guess that
I'd just used the last of
the soap that last Christmas brought

Dear Gran
Many thanks for the hankies
Now I really can't wait for the flu
and the daisies embroidered
in red round the 'M'
for Michael
how
thoughtful of you

Dear Cousin
What socks!
and the same sort you wear
so you must be

the last word in style
and I'm certain you're right that the
luminous green
will make me stand out a mile

Dear Sister
I quite understand your concern
it's a risk sending jam in the post
But I think I've pulled out
all the big bits
of glass
so it won't taste too sharp
spread on toast

Dear Grandad
Don't fret
I'm delighted
So *don't* think your gift will
offend
I'm not at all hurt
that you gave up this year
and just sent me
a fiver
to spend   *Mick Gowar*

AUNTY JOAN

When Aunty Joan became a phone,
She sat there not saying a thing.
The doctor said, shaking his head,
'You'll just have to give her a ring.'

We had a try, but got no reply.
The tone was always engaged.
'She's just being silly,' said Uncle Billy,
Slamming down the receiver enraged.

'Alas, I fear,' said the engineer,
Who was called in to inspect her,
'I've got no choice. She's lost her voice.
I shall have to disconnect her.'

The phone gave a ring. 'You'll do no such
   thing,'
Said Aunty's voice on the line.
'I like being a phone. Just leave me alone,
Or else I'll dial nine-nine-nine!'

John Foster

GRANNY

Through every nook and every cranny
The wind blew in on poor old Granny;
Around her knees, into each ear
(And up her nose as well, I fear).

All through the night the wind grew worse,
It nearly made the vicar curse.
The top had fallen off the steeple
Just missing him (and other people).

It blew on man; it blew on beast.
It blew on nun; it blew on priest.
It blew the wig off Auntie Fanny –
But most of all, it blew on Granny!

Spike Milligan

AUNT CAROL

Making vinegar, Aunt Carol
Fell into her brimming barrel.
As she drowned, my teardrops trickled;
Now she's permanently pickled.

Colin West

FEELING GREAT!

I've been waiting for today.
Grandma's invited us to stay.
Mum wonders if we ought to go.
'Lots of illness round, you know.'

I shall climb Gran's apple trees,
Eat her home-grown strawberries.
Mum thinks I'm looking rather hot.
'It's all right, Mum. Of course I'm not.'

She'll make my favourite cherry cake,
Come fishing with me in the lake.
Mum asks if I'm really sure
I haven't got a temperature.

She'll feed me crusty home-baked bread,
Read me a story on my bed.
'Ought we to choose a later date?'
'Why Mum? What for? I'm feeling great.'

I thought that we were never going.
'Hullo Gran!' But she looks knowing.
'Come close, my lad. What are these
    lumps?'
'I can tell **YOU**! I've got the **MUMPS**!'

Robert Sparrow

BIG AUNT FLO

Every Sunday afternoon
She visits us for tea
And weighs-in somewhere between
A rhino and a flea.
　(But closer to the rhino!)

Aunt Flo tucks into doughnuts,
Eats fruit cake by the tin.
Her stomach makes strange noises
Just like my rude friend, Flynn.
　(Sounds more like a goat, really!)

Then after tea she heads for
The best chair in the room
And crashes on the cushions
With one resounding boom.
　(You'd think a door had slammed!)

Flo sits on knitting needles
And snaps them with a crack.
She squashes dolls and jigsaws
Behind her massive back.
　(And she doesn't feel a thing!)

But Aunt Flo learned a lesson,
There's no doubt about that,
Last Sunday when she grabbed the chair
And sat down on our cat.
　(Big Tom, a cat with a temper!)

The beast let out a
wild yell
And dug his claws
in . . . deep
Poor Flo clutched her
huge behind
And gave a mighty leap.
(She almost reached
the ceiling!)

So now at Sunday teatime
Jam doughnuts going spare.
Dad winks, and asks where Flo is. While Tom
    sleeps on *that* chair.
    (And he's purring, the devil!)

Wes Magee

Have you heard
Of Grans United?
I dare say you haven't,
As they've not been sighted,
All together at a match.
They sit quietly and hatch
Their plans
Behind a barricade,
Of knitting needles;
That's how grans'
Games are won.
Home or away,
Day by day.

The opposition is stiff at times;
Stiff joints – sore bones,
The injuries of extra time.
But they fight back,
With cups of sweet tea,
And bottles of bright capsules;
Games away – by coach to Blackpool,
Internationals, even,
In the cheap Spanish sun;
Bazaars, bingo, television, and toast,
By a warm fireside;
Church choirs and outings,
And, best of all,
Looked-forward-to all week
Visits from beloved grandchildren.
Sweets hoarded in a drawer,
Treasures saved and wrapped in tissue,

Treats and trinkets and surprises;
Secrets shared,
Confidences confided.
I support Grans United.

John Cunliffe

GRANNY GRANNY PLEASE COMB MY HAIR

Granny Granny
please comb my hair
you always take your time
you always take such care

You put me to sit on a cushion
between your knees
you rub a little coconut oil
parting gentle as a breeze

Mummy Mummy
she's always in a hurry – hurry
rush
she pulls my hair
sometimes she tugs

But Granny
you have all the time in the world
and when you're finished
you always turn my head and say
'Now who's a nice girl.'

Grace Nichols

SHED IN SPACE

My Grandad Lewis
On my mother's side
Had two ambitions.
One was to take first prize
For shallots at the village show
And the second
Was to be a space commander.

Every Tuesday
After I'd got their messages,
He'd lead me with a wink
To his garden shed
And there, amongst the linseed
And the sacks of peat and horse manure
He'd light his pipe
And settle in his deck chair.
His old eyes on the blue and distant
That no one else could see,
He'd ask,
'Are we A OK for lift off?'
Gripping the handles of the lawn mower
I'd reply:
'A OK.'

And then
Facing the workbench,
In front of shelves of paint and creosote
And racks of glistening chisels
He'd talk to Mission Control.
'Five-Four-Three-Two-One-Zero –
We have lift off.

This is Grandad Lewis talking,
Do you read me?
Britain's first space shed
is rising majestically into orbit
From its launch pad
In the allotments
In Lakey Lane.'

And so we'd fly,
Through timeless afternoons
Till tea time came,
Amongst the planets
And mysterious suns,
While the world
Receded like a dream:
Grandad never won
That prize for shallots,
But as the captain
Of an intergalactic shed
There was no one to touch him.

Gareth Owen

MY AUNT

I take my Aunt out in her pram
I am her grown-up Nephew 'Sam'!
My Grandma's sister married late
And by a stroke of Life's strange fate
Her children all arrived when we
Were roundabout aged Twenty-three.
It is most pleasing for a chap
To bounce his Aunt upon his lap!

Peggy Wood

I REMEMBER, I REMEMBER

I remember – I remember well –
The first girl that I kissed.
She closed her eyes, I closed mine,
And then – worst luck – we missed!

Anon.

SUZANNA SOCKED ME SUNDAY

Suzanna socked me Sunday,
she socked me Monday, too,
she also socked me Tuesday,
I was turning black and blue.

She socked me double Wednesday,
and Thursday even more,
but when she socked me Friday,
she began to get me sore.

'Enough's enough,' I yelled at her,
'I hate it when you hit me!'
'Well, then I won't!' Suzanna said –
that Saturday, she bit me.

Jack Prelutsky

SHIRLEY SAID

Who wrote 'kick me' on my back?
Who put a spider in my mac?
Who's the one who pulls my hair?
Tries to trip me everywhere?
Who runs up to me and strikes me?
That boy there – I think he likes me.

Denis Doyle

FRIENDS

When first I went to school
I walked with Sally.
She carried my lunch pack,
Told me about a book she'd read
With a handsome hero
So I said,
'You be my best friend.'
After break I went right off her.
I can't say why
And anyway I met Joan
Who's pretty with dark curls
And we sat in a corner of the playground
And giggled about the boy who brought the
    milk.
Joan upset me at lunch,
I can't remember what she said actually,
But I was definitely upset
And took up with Hilary
Who's frightfully brilliant and everything
And showed me her history
Which I considered very decent.
The trouble with Hilary is
She has to let you know how clever she is
And I said,
'You're not the only one who's clever you
    know,'
And she went all quiet and funny
And hasn't spoken to me since.
Good riddance I say
And anyway Linda is much more my type
    of girl;

She does my hair in plaits
And says how pretty I look,
She really says what she thinks
And I appreciate that.
Nadine said she was common
When we saw her on the bus that time
Sitting with three boys from that other
    school,
And I had to agree
There was something in what she said.
There's a difference between friendliness
And being cheap
And I thought it my duty
To tell her what I thought.
Well she laughed right in my face
And then pretended I wasn't there
So I went right off her.
If there's one thing I can't stand
It's being ignored and laughed at.
Nadine understood what I meant,
Understood right away
And that's jolly nice in a friend.
I must tell you one thing about her,
She's rather a snob.
I get the feeling
She looks down on me
And she'll never come to my house
Though I've asked her thousands of times.
I thought it best to have it out with her
And she went off in a huff
Which rather proved my point
And I considered myself well rid.

At the moment
I walk home on my own
But I'm keeping my eyes open
And when I see somebody I consider
    suitable
I'll befriend her.

Gareth Owen

A LITTLE GIRL I HATE

I saw a little girl I hate
And kicked her with my toes.
She turned
And smiled
And **KISSED** me!
Then she punched me in the nose.

Arnold Spilka

SHY LOVE

I remember that disco one Saturday night.
Suddenly seeing the girl for me.
There she sat in the corner like a radial
    piece of light.
Her eyes blue, her hair fair.

She turned around and stared at me.
Her eyes were dazzling and lips were
  flushed.
My heart beat faster
My legs were frozen like a block of ice.

She broke loose from the corner,
And came out fighting on the bell,
And pounded me with her words,
She so forward,
And I so shy.

Then I stunned her.
She fell for the fatal
  blow,
How she wobbled
  to and fro.
There she stood,
  gloves down.
The question came
  out again,
'Do you want
  to dance?'
  I said.

Paul Nice (14)

THE DEATH OF ROMEO AND JULIET

Romeo rode to the sepulchre, 'mong dead
   folks, bats, and creepers;
And swallowed down the burning dose –
   when Juliet opened her peepers.
'Are you alive? Or is't your ghost? Speak
   quick, before I go.'
'Alive!' she cried, 'and kicking too; art thou
   my Romeo?'
'It is your Romeo, my faded little blossum;
O Juliet! is it possible that you were acting
   possum?'
'I was indeed; now let's go home; pa's spite
   will have abated;
What ails you, love, you stagger so; are you
   intoxicated?'
'No, no, my duck; I took some stuff that
   caused a little fit;'
He struggled hard to tell her all, but
   couldn't, so he quit.
In shorter time than't takes a lamb to wag
   his tail, or jump,
Poor Romeo was stiff and pale as any
   whitewashed pump.
Then Juliet seized that awful knife, and in
   her bosom stuck it,
Let out a most terrific yell, fell down, and
   kicked the bucket.

Anon.

POEM

Get your tongue
out
of my mouth;
I'm kissing you
goodbye.

Ted Kooser

THE PRETTY YOUNG THING

A pretty young thing from St Paul's
Wore a newspaper gown to a ball.
   The dress caught on fire
   And burned her attire
Front page, sporting section and all.

Anon.

DON'T CRY, DARLING, IT'S BLOOD ALL RIGHT

Whenever poets want to give you the idea
    that something is particularly meek and
    mild,
They compare it to a child,
Thereby proving that though poets with
    poetry may be rife
They don't know the facts of life.
If of compassion you desire either a tittle or
    a jot,
Don't try to get it from a tot.
Hard-boiled, sophisticated adults like me
    and you
May enjoy ourselves thoroughly with *Little
    Women* and *Winnie-the-Pooh*,
But innocent infants these titles from their
    reading course eliminate
As soon as they discover that it was honey
    and nuts and mashed potatoes instead of
    human flesh that Winnie-the-Pooh and
    Little Women ate.
Innocent children have no use for fables
    about rabbits or donkeys or tortoises or
    porpoises,
What they want is something with plenty of
    well-mutilated corpoises.

Not on legends of how the rose came to
    be a rose instead of a petunia
    is their fancy fed,
But on the inside story of how somebody's

bones got ground up to make
    somebody else's bread.
They'll go to sleep listening to the story of
    the little beggarmaid who got to be
    queen by being kind to the bees
    and the birds,
But they're all eyes and ears the minute they
    suspect a wolf or a giant is going to tear
    some poor woodcutter into quarters or
    thirds.
It doesn't take much to fill their cup;
All they want is for somebody to be eaten
    up.

Therefore I say unto you, all you poets who
    are so crazy about meek and mild little
    children and their angelic air,
If you are sincere and really want to please
    them, why not just go out and get
    yourselves devoured by a bear.

Ogden Nash

THE PEOPLE UPSTAIRS

The people upstairs all practice ballet.
Their living room is a bowling alley.
Their bedroom is full of conducted tours.
Their radio is louder than yours.
They celebrate week-ends all the week.
When they take a shower, your ceilings
    leak.

They try to get their parties to mix
By supplying their guests with Pogo sticks,
And when their orgy at last abates,
They go to the bathroom on roller skates.
I might love the people upstairs wondrous
If instead of above us, they just lived under
  us.

Ogden Nash

TO A SMALL BOY STANDING ON MY SHOES WHILE I AM WEARING THEM

Let's straighten this out, my little man,
And reach an agreement if we can.
I entered your door as an honored guest.
My shoes are shined and my trousers are
  pressed,
And I won't stretch out and read you the
  funnies
And I won't pretend that we're Easter
  bunnies.
If you must get somebody down on the
  floor,
What do you think your parents are for?
I do not like the things that you say
And I hate the games that you want to play.
No matter how frightfully hard you try,
We've little in common, you and I.
The interest I take in my neighbor's nursery
Would have to grow, to be even cursory,

And I would that performing
   sons and nephews
Were carted away with the
   daily refuse,
And I hold that frolicsome
   daughters and nieces
Are ample excuse for breaking leases.
You may take a sock at your daddy's
   tummy,
Or climb all over your doting mummy,
But keep your attentions to me in check,
Or, sonny boy, I will wring your neck.
A happier man today I'd be
Had someone wrung it ahead of me.

Ogden Nash

NEIGHBOURS

We got a new car.
The neighbours got one too.

We painted the house.
The neighbours painted theirs.

We had an extension.
The neighbours had one too.

We moved house.
The neighbours moved
Next door!

Sarah Smith (13)

PLEASE WILL YOU TAKE YOUR CHILDREN HOME BEFORE I DO THEM IN

Please will you take your children home
Before I do them in?
I kissed your little son
As he came posturing within.
I took his little jacket
And removed his little hat
But now the visit's over
So push off you little brat.

And don't think for a moment
That I didn't understand
How the hatchet he was waving
In his grotty little hand
Broke my china teapot
That I've always held so dear –
But would you mind removing him
Before I smack his ear?

Of course I wasn't angry
As I shovelled up the dregs,
I'm only glad the teabags
Didn't scald his little legs.
I'm glad he liked my chocolate cake
I couldn't help but laugh
As he rubbed it in the carpet . . .
Would he like the other half?

He guzzled all the orange
And he guzzled all the Coke –
The only thing that kept me sane
Was hoping he might choke.
And then he had a mishap,
Well, I couldn't bear to look,
Do something for your Auntie little
    sunshine . . .
Sling your hook.

He's been playing in the garden
And he's throttled all the flowers,
Give the lad a marlinspike
He'll sit out there for hours.
I've gathered my insecticides

And marked them with their name
And put them up where children
Couldn't reach them. That's a shame.

Still he must have liked my dog
Because he choked her half to death,
She'll go out for another game
Once she's caught her breath.
He rode her round the garden
And he lashed her with his rope
She's never bitten anyone
But still, we live in hope.

He's kicked the TV now!
I like to see it getting booted
Kick it one more time son
You might get electrocuted!
Yes, turn up the volume,
Twist the knobs, me little treasure
And when the programme's over
There's the door. It's been a pleasure.

Pam Ayres

QUIET FUN

My son Augustus, in the street, one day,
  Was feeling quite exceptionally merry.
A stranger asked him: 'Can you show
    me, pray,
    The quickest way to Brompton
    Cemetery?'
'The quickest way? You bet I can!'
    said Gus,
And pushed the fellow underneath
    a bus.

Whatever people say about my son,
He does enjoy his little bit of fun.

Harry Graham

GROWN UP

Bored by the day,
I decided I'd do something
I hadn't done in years –
go outside and play.
I tried to remember
jump rope games,
the rules of hide and seek,
did you count to forty or a hundred?

I went out and attempted to act naturally.
I hummed a little and kicked a stone
down the street looking for other kids.
They were playing hopscotch.
I showed them marbles
and penny candy and dominoes.
They stared up at me like lilliputians
and said I was too old.

Julia O'Callaghan

THE LIBERATED WOMAN

I'm a liberated woman,
I've even burnt my bra,
I've started eating brown rice,
And I drive a Citroën car.

I've become a vegetarian,
I've given up meat and cigs.
The only bacon I eat now
Is male chauvinist pigs.

I go on protest marches.
I'll travel anywhere
To join a really worthy cause
(If the media is there).

In the pub I drink real ale,
By the pint of course.
Then I go out with the girls
And knock a policeman off his horse.

And when I'm locked up in the nick
With a bunch of lags,
I'll spend all my working day
Sewing 'fe-mail' bags.

Jill M. Batterley (12)

PHYSICAL TRAINING

Our gym-instructress, Miss McPhee,
When gym was over, said to me,
'Stay on, Bill Smith, I'll teach you things.
I'll make you better on the rings,
And after that let's reinforce
Your work upon the vaulting horse.'
I stayed behind. She shut the door.
She'd never been so kind before.
She said, 'So you can get it right
I'll have to hold you very tight.'
She held me here, she held me there,
By gum, she held me everywhere.
She kindly taught me, after that,
To wrestle with her on the mat.
Oh! gosh, the things she taught to me,
Our gym-instructress, Miss McPhee!

Roald Dahl

ACKNOWLEDGEMENTS

The editor and publishers gratefully acknowledge permission to reproduce copyright material by the following authors.

Moira Andrew: 'One Parent Family' from *A Shooting Star* edited by Wes Magee, published by Basil Blackwell 1985. Copyright © Moira Andrew 1985. Reprinted by permission of Moira Andrew.

Joyce Armor: 'Gloria' from *Kids Pick the Funniest Poems* published by Meadowbrook Press. Copyright © Joyce Armor 1991. Used with permission of the author. Reprinted by permission of the publisher.

Pam Ayres: 'Please Will You Take Your Children Home Before I Do Them In' from *Earshot* edited by David Kitchen, published by Heinemann Educational 1988. Copyright © Pam Ayres. Reprinted by permission of Layston Productions Ltd.

Jill M. Batterley: 'The Liberated Woman' from *The Cadbury's Fourth Poetry Book* published by Beaver Books 1986. Copyright © Cadbury's Ltd 1986. Reprinted by permission of the National Exhibition of Children's Art.

James Berry: 'The Barkday Party' and 'Mum, Dad and Me' from *When I Dance* first published by Hamish Hamilton Children's Books. Copyright © James Berry 1988. Reprinted by permission of Hamish Hamilton Ltd.

Phil Bolsta: 'I'm Glad I'm Me' from *Kids Pick the Funniest Poems* published by Meadowbank Press. Copyright © Phil Bolsta 1991. Used with permission of the author. Reprinted by permission of the publisher.

Tony Bradman: 'Down to Earth', 'Never a Dull Moment', 'Starter' and 'The Gerbil' taken from *Smile Please* published by Viking Kestrel and in Puffin Books. Copyright © Tony Bradman 1987. Reprinted by permission of Penguin Books Ltd.

Caryl Brahms. 'Getting Ready for School'. Copyright © Caryl Brahms. Reprinted by permission of the Estate of Caryl Brahms.

William Cole: 'Sneaky Bill' from *A Boy Named Mary Jane*. Copyright © William Cole 1977. Reprinted by permission of the author.

Pie Corbett: 'Grotty Borlotti' from *Another Fifth Poetry Book* edited by John Foster, published by Oxford University Press 1989. Copyright © Pie Corbett 1989. Reprinted by permission of the author.

John Cunliffe: 'Grans United', 'Home Haircut', 'Late Comers', 'Orders of the Day' and 'Telephoning Teacher' from *Standing on a Strawberry* published by Andre Deutsch Children's Books 1983. Copyright © John Cunliffe 1983. Reprinted by permission of Scholastic Publications.

Marcus Holburn: 'Thoughts' from *The Cadbury's First Poetry Book* published by Beaver Books 1983. Copyright © Cadburys Ltd 1983. Reprinted by permission of the National Exhibition of Children's Art.

Julia Holder: 'Lizzie and the Apple Tree'. Copyright © Julia Holder.

Felice Holman: 'The Outlaw' from *At the Top of My Voice and Other Poems* published by Charles Scribner's Sons. Copyright © Felice Holman 1970. Reprinted by permission of Valen Associates Inc.

Zoe Horsley: 'Parents Sayings' from *The Cadbury's Fifth Poetry Book* published by Beaver Books 1987. Copyright © Cadbury's Ltd 1987. Reprinted by permission of The National Exhibition of Children's Art.

Ted Hughes: 'My Uncle Dan' from *Meet My Folks!* published by Faber and Faber Ltd. Copyright © Ted Hughes. Reprinted by permission of the publisher.

David Jackson: 'Irritating Sayings' from *Ways of Talking* edited by David Jackson, published by Ward Lock Educational. Reprinted by permission of the publishers.

Karen Jackson: 'All for an Ice-Cream' from *Ways of Talking* edited by David Jackson, published by Ward Lock Educational. Reprinted by permission of the publisher.

Deepak Kalha: 'Coversations' and 'My Teacher'. Copyright © Deepak Kalha 1988.

X. J. Kennedy: 'Mother's Nerves' from *One Winter Night In August* published by McElderry Books/Macmillan 1975. Copyright © X. J. Kennedy 1975. Reprinted by permission of Curtis Brown Ltd.

David King: 'I Hate Greens' from *A Picnic of Poetry* edited by Anne Harvey, published by Blackie & Sons. Copyright © David King. Reprinted by permission of the author.

David Kitchen: 'Claims', 'Poisoning People is Wrong' and 'What Miss?' from *Earshot* edited by David Kitchen, published by Heinemann Educational 1988. Copyright © David Kitchen 1988. Reprinted by permission of the author.

John Kitching: 'Bored' from *A Third Poetry Book* edited by John Foster, published by Oxford University Press 1982. Copyright © John Kitching 1981. Reprinted by permission of the author. 'Why?' Copyright © John Kitching.

Ted Kooser: 'Poem' from *Evergreen Review*. Copyright © Ted Kooser. Reprinted by permission of the author.

Brenda Leather: 'Ta-ra Mam' from *Home Truths: Writings by North-West Women*. Copyright © Brenda Leather.

James Leggott: 'A Child's Lament' from *The Cadbury's Sixth Poetry Book* published by Beaver Books 1988. Copyright © Cadbury's Ltd 1988. Reprinted by permission of The National Exhibition of Children's Art.